DECORATING with CONFIDENCE

José Wilson and Arthur Leaman, A.I.D.

SIMON AND SCHUSTER • NEW YORK

SBN 671–21518–3
Library of Congress Catalog Card Number: 72-93512
Designed by Betty Crumley
Manufactured in the United States of America
Printed by Lehigh Press, Pennsauken, New Jersey
Bound by American Book-Stratford Press, New York, New York

1 2 3 4 5 6 7 8 9 10

Picture credits:

Alderman Studios 66 bottom, 82 A, 83 F
Wesley Balz 13 bottom, 15
Max Eckert 10 bottom, 13 top, 14, 17, 24, 29, 31, 90 B, 94, 122, 123, 138 A,
    138 B, 138 C, 150 B, 150 C, 158
Erik Falkensteen 150 A, 151
Alexandre Georges 124 bottom
Grigsby 23, 46 A, 74 A, 78 A, 87, 88, 120 C, 148 bottom, 162 bottom
Scott Hyde 40
Lisanti 41 left, 42, 43 bottom, 49 left, 110 bottom, 136 top
Nick de Margolis 41 right
Otto Maya 33 B, 38, 66 top, 75 C, 80, 81, 86, 107 top, 109 top, 110 top, 146
Dennis Purse 139
Ed Rager 22, 48 bottom, 78 C, 103 bottom
Louis Reens 56, 69 top, 72 C, 147
Robert Riggs 10 top, 11, 39 bottom, 53 top, 54 top, 96 A, 104 top, 115 D,
    116 A, 120 B, 134 A, 152, 153
O. Philip Roedel 28 bottom, 113 right
Everette Short 52 top
Ernest Silva, 16, 21, 28 top, 34, 43 top, 46 C, 49 right, 50 top right, 50 bottom,
    51, 55, 57 bottom, 60, 61, 65 left, 72 B, 75 B, 102 left, 104 bottom, 106,
    108, 110 center, 111, 113 left, 116 C, 117, 119, 121, 124 top, 132, 136
    bottom, 145, 156 A, 164 top
Hans VanNes 20, 30, 47, 75 D, 107 bottom, 114 C, 124 top, 137 left.

foreword

Today's shifting social patterns and life styles and greater job mobility have brought about a change in attitude toward the decoration of apartments and houses. There's a restlessness, a desire to experiment, to keep up with the times and enjoy the stimulus of new trends in living. We are increasingly open to innovation and to radical changes of style and design within the field of home furnishings.

Paradoxically, as we try to live larger and more adventurously, modern housing is getting smaller and more standardized, and will become even more so as we move into an age of mass-produced, prefabricated housing necessitated by rising costs in labor and materials. In the not-so-distant future, we'll have to face the challenge of how to give these engineered living units some identity, individuality and warmth. Everyone who has had to cope with the problem of decorating a typical city high-rise apartment or a suburban builder's house knows that you can end up spending more money than you intended just trying to make the place attractive and liveable.

All this requires a more flexible approach to decorating, an ability to decorate for today while thinking of tomorrow. It also means a very realistic appraisal of what you can afford and what you can get for your money, what you can pay someone else to do and what you can tackle yourself. Nowadays it really is easier than ever before to decorate well on a limited budget. You can find an incredible variety and quantity of home furnishings in every price range, and good design from the highest level to the lowest. If you don't want to own your furnishings outright, as many people don't, the answer is the rental package, with monthly payments that can be applied, should you wish, to subsequent purchase.

There has been an equally impressive increase in do-it-yourself materials you can buy in building centers across the country: precut, presized and prefinished paneling, screens, grilles, shelves; self-stick tiles of all types; sheets of acrylic plastic that can be made into shelves or furniture. The manufacturers provide kits with instructions, and they supply leaflets and booklets that tell you not only how to install their products but also all kinds of ingenious ways to use them.

There is so much you can take advantage of that will help you to decorate easily, effectively and inexpensively. What you need to know is where, what and how. The aim of this book is to show you what is available and how you can use it, to give you the inspiration that will spark your ideas, and the know-how to put them into practice, to enable you to get the best return for your decorating dollars.

José Wilson and Arthur Leaman, A.I.D.

contents

more ideas than money   98

Where to shop for good-looking, low-cost furnishings. The advantages of comparison shopping. Fast changes for a room scheme with accent colors and accessories. Do-it-yourself decorating with drip-dry sheets for bedrooms and bathrooms. Transformations of a living room, guest room, bedroom, bathroom, hallway with inexpensive patterned fabrics. Ingenious ways to make a focal point of a bed. Ways to steal space for a work-sewing center, extra closet, laundry, party serving center. Neat solutions for space-shy rooms—niches that hold work in progress, hide a bed, add extra sleeping and seating areas. Decorative deceptions that fool the eye— false beams for a country look, painted *faux bois* on kitchen cabinets, a fireplace "tiled" with a stencil. Simple disguises for off-center windows, unsightly steam pipes, a too-high ceiling, an ugly fireplace. Making space to work at home in a bedroom, living room, a walk-in closet. Clever ways to display commonplace objects. Using a folk art collection as a decorative theme.

self-expression on a shoestring   125

How to get a look that is yours alone in a rental apartment or new house. Improvising a casual or formal dining area. How to make an old-fashioned one-room apartment fit to live in. Starting from scratch in a first apartment. Updating an apartment without extensive redecorating. Solving the studio sleeping problem. Storage you can take with you. Seating arrangements for typical living rooms. Room dividers to redesign floor space. Rugs with a purpose—to define and decorate. Super seating for living rooms—plywood pits and platforms padded with shag carpeting, a giant sweep of sectional sofa units. Using corners to gain space for sleeping, seating, storage. The power of color to direct attention to art, sculpture, a grand piano.

when does it pay to remodel?   149

Rules of thumb for the apartment dweller and house owner. Simple remodeling projects you can undertake yourself. Remodeling an attic, basement, living room or kitchen with color and pattern. Architectural makeover with plywood paneling. Turning a sun porch into an extra living room, a hearth into a party seating and serving shelf. Reviving an old bathroom without changing the fixtures. How to lose an attic and gain a room without expensive structural changes. How to turn a basement into a comfortable family room, teen-age pad or office at home.

fruitful labors   166

The advantages of doing it yourself. Reshaping a room with stripes of paint. Adding ready-made moldings to a plain background. Reviving old furniture with paint and fabric. Stenciling a window shade and a floor. How to fake a four-poster. How to construct a platform. A guide to wall coverings and how to estimate wallpaper yardage. Making your own fabric window shade, vertical blind. Trimming a plain shade. Measuring for window shades and venetian blinds. Diagrams and directions for making a contoured slipcover. How to construct a Parsons table, a cube, a lattice or a fabric-covered frame for a window. Instructions for using sheets to transform a bathroom and to make a round tablecloth—plus a chart of sheet sizes.

where should the money go?

Interesting decoration has always depended more on taste, imagination, an eye for value and a head full of ideas than on money. Decorating snobs slavishly follow current trends and fads, which date as quickly as last year's hemline. Decorating realists know that originality is always in fashion, and it's smarter to be an innovator than to follow the herd.

There are certain guidelines you should follow to avoid getting lost in the seductive bazaar of home furnishings. First, establish a budget and stay within it. Don't overspend on one room and have to skimp on the others. Decide where and how your money will be spent. If you are doing your own decorating, shop around to see what's available within your price range. A few days scouting can save you money and prevent mistakes. Compare prices and don't buy the first thing you see that you like—but don't buy something just because it's cheap, either. Good quality lasts longer and holds up better, so get the best you can afford within your budget.

Cultivate your suppliers. Make friends with salesmen in stores who will tip you off about upcoming sales of furniture and floor coverings. In wall-to-wall carpet, look for remnants and special sales. At a discount of around twenty per cent, sales bring prices down considerably; remnants cost even less and you can often pick up a piece big enough to cover a small room.

Are you better off using an interior designer than trying to do it all yourself? That depends on you. If you know what you like but are unsure of your ability to translate your wishes into decorating schemes, interior designers with their specialized knowledge can save you money because they have all the sources at their fingertips, can get more value for the dollar and know how to solve problems inexpensively. Be honest about what you can afford. Despite what you may have heard, interior designers do stay within the client's budget. Or you might consider working through the decorating department of a store. Check to see that the store carries the kind of furnishings that reflects your taste as you'll be limited to buying everything through it. Ask what the minimum order is and if the design fee is included in the service. Usually it is, provided you purchase the required amount of merchandise, but it's to your advantage to be sure.

Prefinished plywood panels and false beams in rough-hewn finish, good cover-ups for bad walls and ceiling, are within the scope of a competent amateur. So is the stencil on the wood floor that borders a plain area rug with pattern. Rattan and wood furniture, twin floor lamps that eliminate the need for end tables, and a copy of an iron stove are not costly. Designed by Jerome Manashaw, A.I.D., for Du Pont.

INGENIOUS IDEAS FROM INTERIOR DESIGNERS

White painted panels of pierced wood, *opposite top,* the type sold in oriental import shops, become decorative, sound-filtering doors for stereo installation. "Picture" over the mantel is a splashy piece of tie-dyed fabric stretched on an artist's frame sold in art supply stores. Room designed by Gloria Serure.

Plywood frame cut out in a Moorish motif links window with living-room decoration, *opposite bottom.* Shape is outlined with white cord, shade is the same as fabric used on sofa-bed (a foam-rubber mattress on a wood frame with back pad mounted on wood strip attached to wall) and cushions for copies of Victorian wicker chairs. Cut-down table, a Salvation Army bargain, represents a good way to make old, heavily scaled furniture fit into a modern setting. Room designed by Dennis Banchoff.

Wallpaper strips, neatly lined up to meet at right angles on the ceiling, *below,* pull off two decorating tricks—the small room looks higher and larger and more furnished and cozy than it actually is. Regularity of the stripe makes a good backdrop for art. Another height-giver· eye-catching wood construction, hung from the ceiling like a huge fan. Room designed by Louis Bromante, N.S.I.D.

Expert use of color, pattern and texture can make one wall of a room a standout.

Portuguese tile wallpaper in blue, yellow and white brings brightness and eye appeal to the
end wall of a tiny galley kitchen, *above.* The traditional design is an effective background for a
cook's collection of warm-toned copper and wood. Kitchen designed by Michael Brown, N.S.I.D.
Super-graphic swirls of paint on the wall, *opposite top,* take the place of a headboard.
Paint, pillows and Indian lantern concentrate bold color in this one area. Bedside table is an
old sewing-machine base, bought secondhand. Room designed by Robert Braunschweiger.
Stained shutters on the wall near living-room window, *opposite bottom,* mark off a tight little
dining area within a large open-plan room. Pair of Parsons tables and director's chairs
can switch to other parts of the room as needed. Room designed by John Dickenson, A.I.D.
Courtesy Sears.

Another view of the one-wall treatment—a concentration of accessories, plants, posters, objects with varied forms and colors in one area. This is probably one of the easiest and most effective ways to give decorative focus to a small apartment living room where the furniture is fairly modest.

Cluster grouping of plants, accessories and posters behind and above a corner seating arrangement of vinyl-covered sectional sofas, *above,* calls attention to this one area in the type of low-ceilinged, boxy room found in many high-rise apartments. Plastic cubes act as end tables and bookshelves, a small tin trunk turns coffee table, the pillows are covered with Mexican embroideries, fabric remnants. Room designed by Jay Spector. Courtesy Sears.
Built-in storage unit with recessed lighting in lower section, *opposite top,* exposes the handsome face of a stereo system in a manner both decorative and practical. Small graphics fit neatly into the open shelves, plants perch on top of the unit. In the center is a drop-down dining table that when folded back into the wall frees floor space in the living room.
Formica-covered serving shelf with drawers for linens and flatware, *opposite bottom,* is a relatively simple building project that takes the place of a costly, bulky buffet in a dining area where space is at a premium. The wall above is freed for a grouping of prints. Both rooms designed by Max Eckert.

COLOR—THE LEAST EXPENSIVE WAY TO DECORATE

Talented interior designers use imagination and ingenuity to operate within a tight budget.

"**Imagination** means more than dollars any day," says Emily Malino, A.I.D. Her plan for the ultramodern living room, *above*, centers on a dramatic use of one strong color plus shiny surfaces. Terra-cotta carpeting is continued up one wall on a contoured strip of plywood to back a sofa and is graphically outlined with a band of paint and a strip of the same silvered paper that covers the plywood boxes teamed as a multilevel coffee table and end tables. Silvered bulbs with white reflectors, wired through a plywood panel, glitter off the Venetian blinds which have thin slats made of brushed aluminum. Courtesy *Family Circle*.

"**Thrift shops** are great sources for bargain furnishings," says Logan Brown, A.I.D. He picked up all the furniture, lamps and accessories in the sitting room-cum-bedroom, *opposite*, at Goodwill Industries, then painted them in a rainbow of brilliant colors, with the exception of the desk, which was stripped, bleached and pickled. One vivid shade of green on floor, walls, ceiling and bed frame ties together the disparate collection of shapes. The nylon carpeting (it can be bought in strips, as remnants) and the well-designed fabrics are all in the inexpensive category.

Stenciling, a centuries-old paint technique recently revived in updated designs and color combinations, is just about the cheapest way to put pattern on the floor, and has the extra advantage of being easily covered up with another coat of paint whenever you tire of it. The stencil "corridor" that links living and dining areas of this apartment is part of a do-it-yourself kit described on page 169. With the floor carrying the color message, all the simple, lightly scaled furniture (wicker sofa, Parsons tables, Mexican chairs, hanging drawer unit) is kept a noncompetitive white, as are the walls and plywood room divider, coated with a thick stipple paint to promote an aura of cool, Mediterranean freshness. Room designed by Lee Bailey. Courtesy Eastman Chemical.

Painted bands of orange and fuchsia that stripe the natural wood floor and sand-beige wall
of this studio apartment fulfill many decorative functions in the simplest possible way.
The slashes of color provide a visual separation between the sleep-sofa and desk areas and
a coordinating background for a wall-hung grouping of primitive artifacts, while jouncing the
room to life with the stimulus of tones in the red spectrum. These are repeated in a cube
end table, a plinth for one carving, piled-up Indian pillows and tie-dye bedspread (anyone
handy at this technique could make one from plain sheets or muslin). With all this vibrant
color, the room needs a minimum of furniture—light of scale, straight of line, neutral in tone.
Room designed by Josef Head. Courtesy Tyndale, Inc.

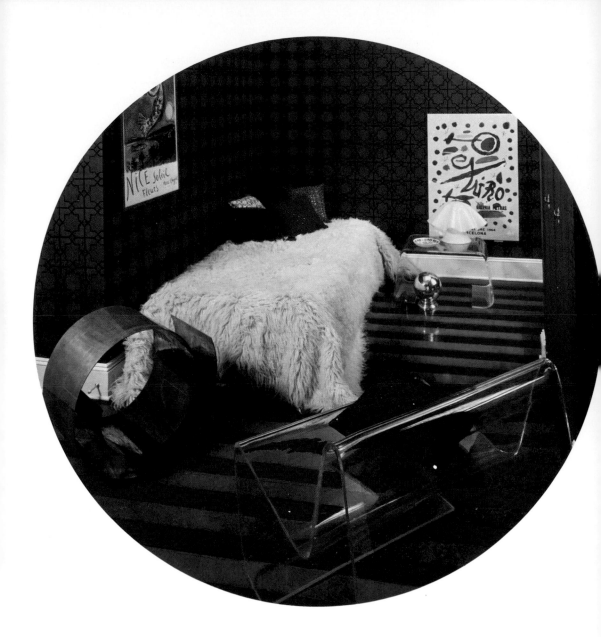

MAXIMUM EFFECTS WITH CONTROLLED COLOR

Pattern predominates in this avant-garde studio pad, *above*. The controlling factor is the use of only two primary colors for the vinyl floor and papered walls, relieved by the white of a sheepskin throw, the no-color of a plastic chair and table, metal sculpture and mercury glass lamp. Furniture is purposely low-down, so the small space will appear larger. Room designed by Jane Victor, N.S.I.D.

Coordination of color in a dining area and adjacent kitchen, *opposite*, comes from the partnership of two fabric-backed vinyl wall coverings. Tile motif vinyl covers the ceiling and island counter, a larger, more decorative floral sheathes the walls. Cool colors are picked up in vinyl floor, laid in stripes, hot tones as accents in red-painted frames of inexpensive chairs and cot that serves as a banquette, with white once more the buffer. Room designed by Shirley Regendahl. Courtesy J. Josephson, Inc.

Dress a bedroom in gingham, all ready-mades by Cameo. Do-it-yourself four-poster
is simply a frame of 2 x 2 pine posts attached to bed frame and baseboard behind the bed, the
hangings four pairs of shirred-back curtains in the same pink-and-white gingham as the spread
and pillow shams. Windows are draped first with sheers, then super-wide curtains in
green-and-white gingham, walls with matching fabric by the yard shirred on rods at floor and
ceiling level. Designed by Arthur Leaman, A.I.D. Courtesy Celanese.

COLOR COMES READY MADE, READY TO USE

When you are decorating a bedroom on a limited budget, some of your best buys are the ready-made curtains and bedspreads, with matching fabric by the yard, that you can find in department stores in a glorious range of colors and patterns, often with a solid-color fabric coordinated to the print. The store will often provide such custom services as making laminated shades from your choice of fabric or making pillows and slipcovers for your furniture, usually at a reasonable cost. While you are shopping around for inspiration, don't overlook tapes and trimmings, one of the quickest and cheapest ways to give a new look to plain curtains and bedspreads.

Block out a border on heavy white antique satin by stitching or ironing on three rows of tape in different colors and a rather dull bedroom becomes enormously stylish. Tapes trim the curtains, valance, bedspread and half-canopy, which is actually just a piece of fabric carried up the wall and draped over two brass curtain rods attached to the ceiling by hooks. The orange of one tape becomes the accent color in the room, the deep charcoal brown of another, the wall color, with everything else the most pristine white. Room designed by R. Holland Trull.

A

B

BUDGET BENEFITS FOR BATHROOMS

Few bathrooms in modern apartments or old houses have much going for them. They are either poky and plain or large and old-fashioned. Don't let that discourage you. With a minimum of cash and an eye for effect, you can give any old bathroom the benefits of color, pattern and unusual touches.

Dormer bathroom, *opposite,* assumes an exotic South Seas ambiance when the walls and slanting ceiling are covered with a see-through bamboo-design wallpaper, windows hung with matching fabric shades, plants allowed to trail unchecked. Add a couple of pleasantly Victorian elements, such as electrified oil lamps, a salvaged washstand (with modern sink inset and linked to plumbing), and a fleecy washable nylon carpet and the makeover is complete. Designed by Cardan Interiors.

Pocket-size powder room, *opposite bottom,* is crammed with amusing odds and ends picked up here and there and assembled with tongue-in-cheek insouciance. Windows are leaded panels from a junk yard, lavatory a Victorian castoff with modern fixtures, chaise percée the kind you buy by mail. Wallpaper, copy of old broadsheets, is reflected in a bevy of little mirrors hung at different angles and levels around the walls. Designed by Cardan Interiors.

Bathroom built-in, *below,* made with plywood, converts the wall opposite the bath into a neat, complete linen storage and makeup area. Practicality is combined wth comfort, for the fluffy synthetic rug is washable, the countertop laminated plastic, the wall coverings washable vinyl and the lining for the niche panels of mirror-surfaced fabric, a recent innovation that has the advantage of being light and easy to install. Designed by Lee Bailey. Courtesy Eastman Chemical.

C

saving graces

As the biggest inflationary rise in any decorating budget is in the cost of labor and professional services, those who save are those who do it themselves. Materials are still reasonably priced, and in the case of the current easy-do products such as pre-cut acrylic plastics and plywood, carpet tiles and stretch fabrics, they are so simple to work with that even a beginner can get good results.

Doing things is not only more profitable, but also more fun than before. Take paint, for instance, always the quickest and cheapest way to give a room a face lift. Think beyond the walls. Paint the floor, stencil a border or accent rug or a window shade, spray-paint furniture in the raw or from the thrift shop. A reliable paint store can tell you what will work best for the job you have in mind and custom-mix the color you want.

Other swift cover-ups are the peel-and-stick papers and vinyls, the vinyls being especially handy because they won't tear and have built-in flexibility. Or you might consider the very inexpensive fabrics you can pick up in mill-end shops, theatrical-supply houses, the dress-goods sections of department and dime stores. Some fabrics sell for as little as 49 cents a yard, so you can afford to buy 100 yards and lavish them all over a small bedroom, for curtains, bedspreads, slipcovers, table skirt. Incidentally, if you buy a whole bolt of fabric, which varies from 30 to 50 yards, you can usually get it at a 10 per cent discount.

At the end of this book are instructions for some really worthwhile do-it-yourself projects. Should you want to attempt something more ambitious, like a painted fantasy finish or découpage, you can take a course or learn by studying one of the excellent books on the subject, some of which are listed on page 183.

Do a lot with a little. Dashing decoration is an amalgam of a stenciled coffee table, inexpensive knock-down furniture, plants, pillows, shelf and supports for painting made of 2 x 5's precut at lumber yard. Designed by Lee Bailey for Eastman Chemical. Stenciled table is work of artist Bill Bell.

Paint is a saving grace when you want a big effect for very little money.

Pick up the pattern of a vinyl wallcovering, repeating the motif on a larger scale in paint as a two-dimensional "accent rug" for a seating group, *opposite top*. Cover with a protective finish or repaint when it wears away. Room designed by Shirley Regendahl. Courtesy J. Josephson, Inc.
Imitate the lattice around a bedroom window in an oversized-trellis stenciled floor, color-matched to the yellow-and-white fabric, *opposite bottom*. Achieving this low-cost look of wall-to-wall carpeting takes a weekend (see directions, page 168). Room designed by Ruth Adams. Courtesy *House Beautiful*.
Attach moldings to a ceiling painted a light shade, then use a deeper color between them to give the impression of projecting beams, *below*. If you are artful with a paint brush, you might cover a wood dining table, self-made buffet shelf and supports with a fantasy finish. Flame-stitch fabric is a chic replacement for vinyl slings on director's chairs. Designed by Hamilton-Howe.

Stripe a floor with three colors of vinyl, *opposite,* then continue the pattern in paint up the window shade and wall and around the ceiling light to add the punch of an abstract painting to a conventional white kitchen. Refrigerator may also be spray-painted fire-engine red, making a virtue of a necessity. Kitchen designed by Ethel Samuels, N.S.I.D.

Paint the walls of a small room, *top,* with panels of blue and yellow to make a fresh and vibrant background for dining. Painted trim can fake the appearance of a corner cabinet, frame an assemblage of objects hung on one deep-blue painted panel. Room designed by Max Eckert.

Color a piece of found furniture such as a useful but cumbersome Victorian chest, *bottom,* the same shade as the walls and it will fade into the background. Strong red unifies the mixture of accessories and patterns, a good trick for a one-room apartment. Room designed by Allen Stuart, A.I.D.

A

FACE LIFTS FOR FURNITURE

Even the dreariest secondhand castaways can look quite snazzy if you hide their defects with pattern.

Cover cubes of corrugated paper or cardboard and a table put together from packing boxes with vinyl-treated papers, A, and you've got it made—with a few hours' work. Courtesy Wallcovering Industry Bureau.

Paste a paper dado along the wall, top with a plastic molding, then cover the drawer fronts of standard chests with the same paper and paint them a matching color for a quick way to refurbish a young girl's bedroom, B. Room designed by Carl Steele of Kunzig & Steele.

Transform a beat-up chest by gluing a leopard-print fabric over it, then outlining the drawers and top with black lacquer, C. For fabric-gluing instructions, see page 167. Or you could use peel-and-stick paper of a suitable pattern. Room designed by William Welsh.

Take a plywood pedestal, cover it with the same pre-pasted strippable vinyl used on the walls, add a clear acrylic plastic top and you've got a perfect plinth for your pet piece of art, D. One of the saving graces of strippable papers is that they just peel off if you make a mistake in alignment and won't tear while you do it. Courtesy Wallcovering Industry Bureau.

B

C D

FABRIC FOR A FAST COVER-UP

There's almost nothing you can't do with fabric—glue it, drape it, shirr it, staple it to a frame. Capitalize on the inexpensive, well-designed and color-coordinated fabrics and ready-mades sold in department stores and create a room scheme that looks as if it was designed just for you.

Strew a flock of patterns, similar in coloring but different in design, over a bedroom, *above.* Bedhead panel is fabric-by-the-yard twin of bedspread; curtains are the same print, sans daffodils; ceiling matches the pattern on the chair cushion. Room designed by Virginia Frankel for Celanese.

Lavish a printed fabric, cheap enough to be used freely (under $3 a yard), on a room, *opposite top,* for a penny-wise look of luxury. To cover walls and replace curtains, shirr fabric on rods. White cube tables, white-painted furniture and white vases keep the look light. Courtesy Bloomcraft. Designers: Denning & Fourcade.

Take a single print in paper and fabric as a restful background for repose, *opposite bottom.* Shirr fabric on frames of built-in storage unit, make tie-back bed curtains. Courtesy Burlington Industries.

Ticking breaks out of its blue-and-white-striped prison at long last, redesigned by Oscar de la Renta in luscious colors and patterns, sold by the yard as a match-mate to mattresses by Simmons, the bed people.

Cloud formations in water-color blues and greens waft across mattress and foundation set on a blue-carpeted platform, *above*. Matched fabric makes bedhead panel, slipcovers chairs and wastebasket.

Folk-art forms of birds and geometrics riot all over a bedroom, *opposite top*, from mattress and throw to screen panels, valance, lamp shades, pillows, even the mat of a picture over the bed.

Bouquets of flowers start to bloom on a mattress and spread around the bedroom and its adjoining dressing area, *opposite bottom*. Home sewers can run up fabric by the yard into the dust ruffle, bed canopy, night-table skirt, dressing-room curtains and valance.

SCREENS THAT HIDE

You can count on a screen for a quick disguise, a decorative coverall, an impermanent wall.

Screen a kitchen from an open-plan living room, *above,* with a divider of hinged prefinished plywood panels attached to ceiling and side wall. Apply moldings to panels and walls for a unified background. (For how to apply moldings, see page 166.) The bonus: oodles of extra space to display art. Room designed by David Barrett, A.I.D.

Back a bed with the kind of small inexpensive oriental screen you find in import shops, *opposite top,* and you have a space-saving, off-beat stand-in for a headboard. Courtesy Springs Mills, Inc.

Put up a false front of hinged screens attached to a ceiling track, *opposite bottom,* and you gain both a wall and space behind for a small dressing area. Room designed by Louis Bromante, N.S.I.D.

Block out a niche for an important painting at one end of a boxy apartment living room with twin free-standing screens made of hardboard (less weighty to shift around than plywood) with double-acting hinges. For a feeling of space, cover one side of the screens with a reflective silver-foil paper or mirror-surfaced fabric, *top.* Staple textured fabric to the other side, *bottom,* and you get a totally different shape and effect when the screens are reversed flat against the walls. Room designed by Jack Lenor Larsen, A.I.D. Courtesy Allied Chemical.

SCREENS THAT DIVIDE

The ability of a screen to define and divide space is one of its greatest assets, especially in rental apartments where a more permanent installation is inadvisable. Screens may be bought or made from precut plywood, hardboard and the kind of ready-made pierced panels sold in lumber yards or import shops—plus, of course, the essential hinges and sliding tracks.

Close off a kitchen from an apartment dining area, *above left,* with stock panels of cut-out plywood, painted and backed with sheets of translucent plastic in a color that blends with the room scheme. Panels slide open or closed in two tracks. Room designed by Tom Ashjean, A.I.D. Courtesy *Better Homes & Gardens.*

Shield an open-plan living room from the entrance, *above right,* without blocking the light by making a simple frame of 2 x 2's to hold a pair of mashrabiyyah, the Arab-influenced pierced wood panels that you can buy in import shops. Room designed by Jack Davidson.

FOCUS ON A WALL

Wealthy art collectors orient a room to a huge abstract canvas. Follow the same principle in a more modest way by devoting one wall to something personal, dramatic or fun, such as a blown-up poster or print, a paper mural or your own art work. It's easy, effective and only costs a few dollars.

Splash a super-graphic over the wall of a one-room apartment or a family room, *above*, bringing the door into the picture by pasting one section over it. This type of pop-art mural, in paper or vinyl, can be ordered through wallpaper stores. Room designed by Delphene Richards, N.S.I.D. Courtesy *Family Circle*.
Blow up a poster of your particular passion, be it the Beatles or the Royal Ballet, to a giant black-and-white photo mural, *opposite top*. Photographic studios do this kind of work, charging according to size. Room designed by Larry Peabody, A.I.D., for Allied Chemical.
Mass photographs of your family and friends or your travel shots in a symmetrical wall arrangement, like a picture grouping, *opposite bottom*. You can frame them yourself with sectional metal strip kits that come in different sizes. Room designed by Delphene Richards, N.S.I.D. Courtesy *Family Circle*.

PUT UP A SOUND BARRIER

As every high-rise apartment dweller soon discovers, when walls are thin, noise is a perpetual headache. Before going in for costly soundproofing, consider some ingenious ways to baffle your neighbors.

Pad the walls of a small room where you crave quiet for working, reading or listening to music, *above left,* with a heavy, closely woven fabric that soaks up sound. For easy removal, put up fabric with strips of Velcro tape. In a bachelor apartment or home office, a neutral herringbone suiting, coordinated with pebble-pattern nylon carpet, provides a non-distracting background for a collection of oil paintings. Room designed by Jerome Manashaw, A.I.D., for Du Pont.
Tile a wall with panels of self-sticking squares of cork (one of the best of all insulators), alternating them with panels of mirror tiles for a lighter, brighter effect, *above right*. Both cork and mirror tiles are 12 inches square, cost only about $9 a dozen and are easily installed by an amateur handyman. Cork background also provides a pin-up surface for prints. Courtesy Sears.
Carpet the walls as well as the floor, *opposite top,* to turn your apartment into a cozy, peaceful cocoon. It's an easy do-it-yourself project. If your ground color is solid, pick a pattern like this wavy, vibrant shag carpet with the appeal of a modern tapestry for the wall areas. Courtesy Sears.
Fabricate a false wall for your bedroom, where noise is the worst problem, *opposite bottom,* by padding a row of screens with thin layers of foam rubber and stretch fabric. Concertina placement that creates sound-absorbing pockets of air is much more effective than a flat surface. To link wall to room scheme, slipcover bed bases in same stretch fabric. Room designed by Lee Bailey for Eastman Chemical.

A

B

C

D

BRIGHTEN YOUR BACKGROUND

If a plain, pale wall is anathema to you, even if your home is a rented apartment, you don't have to settle for the paint the landlord provides. Nowadays, with papers strippable and fabrics easy to attach and detach, you can have just about any kind of look you crave.

Dramatize one wall with a strong, vibrant color such as tomato-red felt attached with Velcro tape against which you can display books and accessories, *opposite A*. Paper the other walls with a print, integrate the window with ready-made shutters backed with matching fabric, which you might also use to slipcover a small upholstered chair. Courtesy W & J Sloane, New York.

Throw light on a dark inner room, *B*, with a shimmering strippable foil paper that comes in a range of cool-to-warm metallic tones—silver, platinum, gold, copper and bronze. Accentuate the shiny-surfaced look with vinyl upholstery and pillows. Courtesy General Tire & Rubber Co.

Make an entrance into a stunning gallery for art with false walls of aluminum roofing panels screwed to wood strips or the ceiling molding, *C*. This bargain basement version of the ultra-chic stainless steel wall costs under $3.50 for each 25¼-inch by 8-foot panel. Courtesy Sears.

Liven up a family room with a shiny super-star vinyl, a blaze of red, white and blue, *D*. Bulletin board becomes an ever-changing montage of everyone's favorite posters. Courtesy Amtico.

ALL DONE WITH MIRRORS

Mirrors work miracles, making cramped spaces seem twice as large, twice as bright, as they really are.

Mirrored planter, *above left,* is a much more successful way to show off house plants in a small entrance than to stand them against the plain wall. Planter can be built of 2 x 4's and stained, then filled with white pebbles for drainage. To encourage growth without natural light, special bulbs for plants can be installed in the down lights. Designed by Tom Ashjean, A.I.D. Courtesy *Better Homes & Gardens*.

Mirrored sculpture, *above right,* stands out against a dark wall in a narrow hallway. For this form of creative art, you buy the units, assemble them as you please. Mirror sculpture by Beylerian. Courtesy Celanese.

Mirrored panels, *opposite top,* less expensive than a completely mirrored wall, give sense of width and space to a small dining area. Room designed by Peg Walker. Courtesy Window Shade Manufacturers Assn.

Mirrored background, *opposite bottom,* that adds fantastic glitter to a conversation group is all done with mirror tiles from Sears. Super-strips of tiles are taped to walls within white-painted furring, more tiles cover square and rectangular plywood platforms for étagères (for directions, see page 171).

Put pattern on the kitchen floor, *above left,* with special nylon carpeting in a dimensional cane design that makes a small crowded area look larger. Courtesy Du Pont.

Continue carpeting up the wall, *above right,* and over a window seat to provide an upholstered banquette with built-in cushion (carpet underlay of high-density polymeric foam molds to contours of stairs or seating platforms, also has soundproofing qualities that make it a good acoustical cover for walls).

Carpet the terrace, *below,* with the same tough indoor-outdoor floor covering as in the living room. Resilient foundation of carpeting resists heat, moisture and mildew. Both designed by Carole Frankel for the Olin Corporation.

FLOORS THAT CAN TAKE IT

Embellish a plain floor with a vinyl facsimile of the cool and colorful ceramic tiles of Spain and Portugal, *above*. Appropriate for a room that gets lots of traffic from outdoors, these tiles are easy to clean and a cinch to install with double-faced tape. Room designed by Margaret White. Courtesy Celanese.

WINDOW DRESSING THAT PAYS OFF

Cover a pair of windows, *top,* with thin-slat brushed-aluminum Venetian blinds outlined with self-adhesive aluminum tape on the window frame, then bridge them with two mirrored screens, and the boxiest apartment living room will seem wider and more elegant. One blind can conceal the air conditioner while letting air circulate. Courtesy *Family Circle.*

Filter strong sunlight beamed through a window wall opening onto a terrace, *bottom,* with vertical louvers of translucent white shade-cloth strips that you can install using the system on page 174. Designed by Albert Herbert, A.I.D. Courtesy Window Shade Manufacturers Assn.

Tie together a series of windows that are awkwardly placed by running lattice panels on sliding tracks across the entire wall, *opposite top,* then hang inexpensive synthetic sheers behind them. Stock panels of this kind can be purchased at lumber yards. See page 179 for directions on framing a window with lattice. Room designed by Gertrude Schnee.

Control light in a small bedroom with a combination of shutters and black-out shades, *opposite bottom.* Simple framework around the window hides structural beams and adds a bank of shelves for storage. Room designed by Emily Malino, A.I.D. Courtesy Window Shade Manufacturers Assn.

SEE WHAT'S HAPPENED TO THE PLAIN OLD SHADE

If you don't care for the fussiness or upkeep of curtains, but want color and pattern at your windows, you're in luck. You can get bamboo or Venetian blinds in color, patterned shades, shades laminated to fabric, even painted shades. Should you want a very special color or design and are moderately skilled with a paintbrush, you can even execute the artwork yourself. For how-to on window shades see pages 168, 172–73, 174–75, 180.

Bamboo blinds, undeniably practical but seldom esthetically exciting, can now be bought in a most sophisticated tortoiseshell finish, *opposite top,* that blends beautifully with warm colors and wood tones. If you are weary of an uninspiring view or uninteresting windows, build and stain a frame of plywood arches to cover the whole wall and hang a series of blinds behind them. Room designed by Joan Spiro.

Venetian blinds once came only in white or sickly pastels, not the brilliant colors of today. For a small workroom or home office with one tiny window, *opposite bottom,* you might extend the wall by building out a frame of plywood strips and then hanging colorful blinds over the window and at either side to hide office-supply storage. Courtesy Stanley Furniture.

Window shades are like canvases—take plain shade cloth and you can paint it in a free-form design and show it off as all your own work, *above.* This is a marvelous way to bring color and design to a glass-walled corner apartment in a high-rise where there is precious little wall space for displays of art, and of course the shade also fulfills the more pedestrian function of blocking light. Extra-wide shades hung on heavy-duty rollers to fit large windows can be made to order. Room designed by John Van Koert. Courtesy Window Shade Manufacturers Assn.

LOOK ON LIGHT
AS A DECORATIVE SOURCE

Lighting is no longer just something to see by but one of the most important elements of present-day decorating, a simple yet enormously versatile way to change the mood of a room.

Project light pictures on the ceiling or walls of a living room kept as blankly white as a movie screen for just this purpose, *opposite*. Slides changed according to mood at the flick of a switch represent the newly popular low-cost substitute for paintings and pattern. Room designed by C. Ray Smith.

Light up the base of a coffee table, *top,* by laying two square sheets of glass over an ingenious assemblage of eight plastic balls illuminated from inside. This is part of the modern trend to furniture that is also a low-level light source. Room designed by William Welsh of Bloomingdale's.

Hide light under a bed by screwing tubular lamps to the frame, *center,* which makes this solid piece of furniture seem to float. Carpeting that undulates up the bed wall like a wave is made of an iridescent blue fiber that reflects the soft light, creating a perfect mood for sleeping or relaxing. Room designed by John Elmo, A.I.D. Courtesy Allied Chemical.

Let light become art by interspersing inexpensive dime-store lamps, plugged into multiple outlets, and crystal and silvered accessories on twin metal étagères, *bottom,* an intriguing and unusual idea that sparks a scintillating radiance. Photographed at Celanese House.

Combine different types of lighting to accentuate the striking shapes of an African art collection, *opposite top*. Modern circular chandelier with tiny bulbs beams soft light over dining table. Spotlights on track and down lights inset in ceiling pinpoint masks and sculptures in dining-sitting room. Smaller objects in the wall niche are thrown into relief by recessed tubular lighting fixture. Room designed by Vladimir Kagan. Courtesy Champion-International.

Focus light on one wall by assembling a series of stacked white Plexiglas rectangular pedestals, illuminated from within, alternating with Plexiglas shelves, *opposite bottom*. This tremendously effective, updated version of the display wall for art and accessories can be easily put together with inexpensive components you can buy or make yourself. Courtesy Tyndale, Inc.

Stack lighted lanterns ziggurat fashion to create a glowing column of paper sculpture, *above*. Another type of inexpensive Akari paper lantern stands on a chest. Courtesy Bloomingdale's.

investing in
furniture

Furniture will always take the biggest bite out of your decorating budget, but
there are ways to economize. One is to buy dual purpose pieces: table-desks,
lightly scaled pull-up chairs that can switch from the dining to the conversation
area, a sleep-sofa, storage cubes or chests of end-table height.

In upholstered furniture, get the best you can afford. Quality and good
workmanship are worth every penny. Sofas and chairs cost less in muslin, so
look for those with straight or sculptural lines and loose cushions that you
can cover yourself with stretch fabrics and knits. Though most living rooms

need a major seating piece, it doesn't have to be a big sofa. You may be better off with a pair of love seats, or sectionals that can be used together or apart.

Places to bargain-hunt are shops that advertise sales of decorator showroom samples (not subject to return, so check carefully), manufacturers' outlets, department-store warehouse sales and sales of floor samples and model-room furniture.

Modern furniture is the greatest value on the market today. The latitude in design and price is fantastic and the simple, classic lines look well anywhere. Also consider modern or traditional knock-down furniture kits you assemble or finish yourself and, of course, used furniture. There are many ways to salvage an old piece. If you strip off superfluous detail and give it a coat of paint, it will look like considerably more than you paid for it. For how-to on painting furniture see page 167.

Buy upholstered furniture of the moderately priced department store type in muslin, then cover it in your choice of fabrics according to the look you want. For a modern scheme in dark to light neutrals, *below,* an overscaled contemporary print teams with a small geometric in beige and off-white and a solid brown. Smaller pieces have chrome underpinnings. Traditional interpretation in yellow, gray and white, with the same sofa and club chairs, *opposite,* combines floral, striped and plain fabrics, wood and lacquered finishes. All fabrics are 60-inch-wide Fortrel knits that have no pattern distortion as they won't pull out of shape. (See pages 176–77 for how to make slipcovers with knit fabrics.) Designed by David Holcomb, A.I.D., for Celanese.

ONE ROOM, TWO STYLES

Bedrooms in modern apartments and houses are often so small and standard-ized that to give them any style or individuality without overspending takes some decorating know-how. The two main elements you have to work with are pattern and furniture, and by combining these cleverly you can create any mood or effect you want, as you can see in the bedrooms on these pages, which are identical in architecture, furniture placement, even the pattern of the sheets used for window and bed treatments, yet completely different in style and overall impression.

Conventional bedroom, *opposite,* has the cozy, frilly charm of a nineteenth-century boudoir. The lines are rounded, curving, from the love seat and slipper chair covered in dotted stretch fabric to the white-painted turned-wood table, Chinese garden seat topped with a circle of glass, even the silvered shell collection. The ruffles on the tie-backs and bed are cut from a pink-and-red floral sheet, color-coordinated to the op-art pattern sheet used for the curtains and bed treatment. **Contemporary bedroom,** *above,* features straight and sculptural lines and swirling patterns in the current idiom. The seating pieces are sectionals with plain stretch upholstery over foam, the window shades and bed treatment tailored, the walls covered with marbleized paper, the collection, treenware. Mirrorlike reveal and valance around the windows are made from sheets of chrome that can be cut to size. Both rooms designed by Lee Bailey for Eastman Chemical.

Before you invest in furniture, consider carefully the type you really prefer—traditional or modern. Because of the workmanship involved, traditional costs more, even in reproductions, so you may be better off with an eclectic mixture of old and new. Or you can assemble your rooms in stages, each year replacing a secondhand or inexpensive make-do with one really good reproduction.

Mix your periods for a more livable, less formal room scheme, perhaps combining a center conversation group of contemporary sectional sofas, *opposite top,* with eighteenth and nineteenth century reproductions. As the latter, with the exception of the Empire-style commode, are lightly scaled and open in design, the room, though fully furnished, does not look crowded. Room designed by Barbara D'Arcy of Bloomingdale's.

Pick one style you really go for, such as American Colonial, which can be used throughout a bedroom, *opposite bottom,* where the heavily scaled pieces are appropriate, but not overwhelming. Add inexpensive extras of the same stamp: readymade curtains and bedspread in patchwork fabric, secondhand foot locker, old-fashioned prints and mirrors. Designed by Ruth McLeod of *Bride's Magazine.* Courtesy Syroco.

Opt for plastic furniture if you want a very sleek contemporary room with a minimum outlay of cash, *above left.* As a substitute for a second sofa (and a less costly alternate) you might build a seating platform across one end of the room, cover it with the carpeting and pad it with lots of bright little accent pillows. Room designed by Peg Walker. Courtesy J. Josephson, Inc.

Mail-order your furniture. It's perfectly possible. Sears, for one, sells good design of all periods in a wide price range and if you aren't near a retail store you can select from their catalogue. Examples of what's available are the chrome director's chairs with flowered slings, modern sofa, chrome and glass coffee table and Parsons end table shown *above right.*

At any price, the best way to get an interesting and personal room scheme is to mix furniture styles, finishes and textures. True, it's a challenge to your eye and your imagination, but much more rewarding than clinging to the old cliché room done in an uninspired matched "suite" of furniture.

Keep it simple in design and you can successfully associate wildly disparate styles, *opposite top,* from a semicircular sofa, tubular metal chair and plastic plinths of the Seventies and a Twenties straight-lined shiny white lacquer side table to a marbleized Empire occasional table and a lovely old Provincial pine armoire. Room designed by Carl Steele of Kunzig & Steele.

Pull together a mélange of different patterns, textures and designs with a unifying theme, such as a safari motif picked up in a zebra rug, fake fur pillows, antlers and animal figures, *opposite bottom.* The furniture, apart from the straight-lined sleep sofa and chestnut sofa table, is the kind you can pick up in import shops—Mexican wood and rawhide chair, wicker hamper turned coffee table. Courtesy Sanitas.

Be offbeat in your approach. For a dining area, reproduction Queen Anne chairs look refreshingly different with an up-to-the-minute lacquered wood and chrome table, *below.* Host and hostess wing chairs can switch to the seating area, the table can double as a work desk. Room designed by Lee Bailey for Eastman Chemical.

A ROUNDUP OF CONTEMPORARY DESIGN

If modern furniture turns you on, count your blessings. Advanced techniques of injection molding and lamination have brought down production costs to the point where you can find plenty of good-looking, soundly constructed furniture in wood, molded plywood and plastic within the budget price range.

Molded plastic sleep-sofa, tables and chairs imported from Italy by Simmons are well-designed, lightweight and washable, *opposite top.* For a change of color scheme, all you have to do is slipcover the sofa cushions with a different fabric.

Quick-change sofas by Kroehler work on a brand-new principle that eliminates the need for cleaning upholstery, *opposite center.* The synthetic tailored covering that wraps around the frame is attached with Velcro, so it can be stripped off for machine washing as easily as peeling a banana. There's a bonus: you can order a second cover with the sofa as a seasonal replacement, or just for a change of pace. For details, see page 176.

Trend-setting furniture of two types combined in a room designed by William Welsh of Bloomingdale's, *opposite bottom.* Undulating sculptural forms of lightweight foam chairs, loveseat and ottoman from Italy, covered in tomato-red stretch fabric, contrast with angular frames of laminated wood desk, chests and open armchairs lacquered in vivid tangerine, plum and red.

Butcher blocks turned tables are some of the biggest bargains in furniture today. Dining-cum-work table with thick maple top, massive wood legs, *top,* may be ordered in different lengths and widths. Another butcher-block top makes a wall-hung serving shelf; to the left is the original type of butcher's chopping block, with a top 12 inches thick. Dining room designed by Joel Grey.

Blow-up furniture by Quasar in clear or colored plastic, *center,* is deflatable, so it presents no moving problem. Table has a light column in the center. Repair kit is included with the furniture in case of mishaps.

Futuristic molded plywood chairs cushioned by upholstered foam rubber are the new, sleek versions of the easy chair, *bottom.* In dining area behind them are modern reinterpretations in chrome of eighteenth-century bamboo armchairs with matching table. Furniture by Flair, Inc.

CAN YOU BELIEVE IT'S CARDBOARD?

Cardboard and paper furniture has finally made the design grade. The latest versions are not only light, cheap and versatile, but also comfortable and good-looking enough to be an asset to any room.

Laminated layers of corrugated cardboard are molded into straight or sinuous shapes (strong enough to support an economy car) for the Easy Edges collection, a revolutionary breakthrough in furniture design. There are pieces for all rooms, ranging from a $25 stool to a $120 large dining table, and the textured, suedelike beigey-brown surface is said to be enhanced by use. In the room *above,* designer Barbara D'Arcy of Bloomingdale's combined the furniture with edgeboard sections on floor and walls to create a total soft-monotone environment. Four of the chairs, lined up, make a sectional sofa.
Paper tubes and plastic joints unite to form a new type of knockdown furniture by Environmental Concepts, Inc. Called Set-Ups, the group consists of different tables, chairs, a desk, étagère and canopy bed, *opposite,* in a color range of white, black, brown, red and yellow. The furniture for a whole room can be assembled in minutes, without tools, by slipping the tubes into the joints, adding plastic tops, shelves and slings. The low cost (from $12.95 for a stool to under $40 for the étagère), convenience and mobility make this a good candidate for a first apartment, college dormitory or a weekend house, as the disassembled furniture can be easily moved by car.

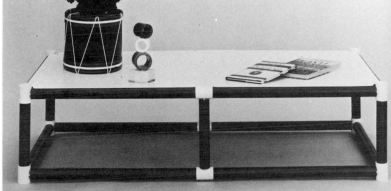

A

B

C

FURNITURE YOU CAN HAVE BOTH WAYS

That hardy breed of furniture known as leisure, or indoor-outdoor, is a smart investment because it wears well inside or out and has a lightness and simplicity that looks right almost anywhere. Wrought iron, cast aluminum, plastic, tubular steel, wicker and rattan are some of the materials, with ageless wicker especially favored for its low cost, adaptability and availability. There's almost nothing you can't find in wicker, from sofas to chests to headboards, and its airy grace makes it a good choice for small apartments and houses. The Hong Kong copies of fancifully lacy Victorian wicker pieces sold by import shops and mail-order houses are particularly fetching.

Choose wicker if you are furnishing a bedroom on a budget. You can leave it the natural tone or spray-paint it to match your color scheme. Here, in bedroom A, wicker teams with another decorative money-saver, drip-dry sheets. Three double sheets are all it takes to cover a pair of window screens, chair cushions, window seat pad, valance and shades (just buy adhesive-backed shade cloth, cut to size, peel off backing and iron on fabric). Courtesy West Point Pepperell.
Count on airy bamboo, reinterpreted in durable aluminum, to furnish a tiny dining area without a feeling of crowding, B. Four chairs, matching glass-topped table and étagères fit in easily. Room designed by Shirley Regendahl. Furniture by Meadowcraft. Courtesy J. Josephson, Inc.
Take six stools, woven in Portugal, add a sheet of glass on two plastic cylinders for a table, C, and you have a combination seating and low-level dining setup for almost no money.
Spray wicker white to cool off a sun porch, D, then sheathe everything in drip-dry striped sheets run horizontally on seat pads, vertically at windows to give the room height. Valance is made from cotton tassels and jumbo dots cut from sheet side panels. Courtesy Burlington Industries.

D

A

THE LIGHT RELIEF OF PAINTED FURNITURE

With a lick of paint, a piece of plain or secondhand furniture can become a colorful accent piece and a revitalizer for a dull room. Found furniture sources: thrift shops, auctions, garage and rummage sales, church bazaars, the Salvation Army, even the streets if you live in a city where people put out their discards for collection. Raw wood furniture sold by department stores, lumber yards, mail-order houses and unpainted furniture stores is always cheaper than the finished article.

Create a color scheme by spraying wicker furniture lemon yellow, a Parsons table glossy black, then spatterdashing the floor in yellow and white on black, A. Room designed by Joan Lerrick.
Outline a design with masking tape on the fronts of two stacked unpainted chests, slightly overlapping, then fill it in with paint, B, for a slick graphic look that ties the simple case pieces into the contemporary room scheme. Room designed by Donald Cameron for Celanese House.
Stripe the fronts of three wall-hung chests, blocking out the varying widths with masking tape and then painting them in four tones of one color, C. Add decorative handles and you have a piece of furniture striking enough to become the focal point of the room, with the addition of a painting and accessories. Room designed by Carl Steele of Kunzig & Steele.
Paint a rainbow of parfait colors on the sides and ladder rungs of a bunk bed, D, and it acts as a bright dividing line between two children's identical play areas, each with a painted bentwood chair and Parsons table. Room designed by Jane Victor, N.S.I.D.

B

C

D

A

B

A. Latest version of the perennial director's chair has a folding frame lacquered in a choice of colors, matching vinyl slings.
B. Mass-produced copy of the famous Breuer side chair displays the characteristic cantilevered chrome-plated frame, seat and back of black-painted wood and natural cane.
C. Handcrafted tub chair from Mexico of rope and rawhide, pigskin over roughhewn wood can be left in its natural rustic state or painted to match your color scheme.
D. Classic bentwood armchair with cane seat now comes with the frame in colors as well as the more customary wood finish.
E. Contoured ABS molded plastic chair can be bought in white or bright orange.
F. Pull-up armchair has a one-piece vinyl seat and back, a chrome-plated frame.

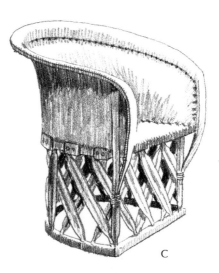

C

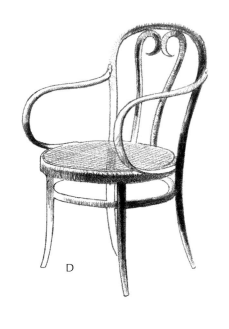

D

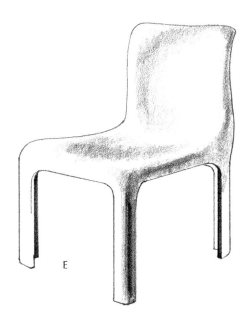

E

F

THE DESIGN IS FINE,
THE PRICE IS RIGHT

Remember the days when the butterfly chair was just about the only good cheap seat around? Now there are so many good-looking inexpensive chairs that you're just, as likely to find them on the terrace of a millionaire (who knows a bargain when he sees one) as in a young couple's first apartment, for nowadays good design is the common denominator of taste. The chairs shown here all cost less than $50, some less than $15, depending on where you buy them.

A

B

C

E   F

TWO LOW-COST CLASSICS

Now so familiar that it is hard to believe it wasn't always with us, the Parsons table (a graduate of the Parsons School of Design) is perhaps the most versatile and widely used of all modern pieces of furniture. Cheap to buy, even cheaper to make (for directions, see page 178), this straight-lined table may be covered with laminated plastic, lacquer, fabric, paper, vinyl, or a fantasy finish.

The equally versatile cube comes in all kinds of materials—wood, plastic, paper, cardboard—different sizes and finishes, and its uses are almost too numerous to mention.

Parsons dining table, A, with laminated plastic surface is perfectly at home in a traditional setting with imported rush-seated country chairs. Room designed by Joan Lerrick. Courtesy Magee.
Versions of the Parsons table in different sizes and shapes, wood-grain or lacquered finishes, B, serve as coffee or end tables, side or serving table. Courtesy Tyndale, Inc.
Twin Parsons tables, long and narrow, separate to form a corner work area, C, or may be pushed together lengthwise to provide dining space for six. Courtesy Celanese.
Add-a-cube arrangements can be put together like building blocks in groups or stacks to suit your needs and space. Four cubes in a walnut finish team to make a low square corner table, D. Subtract one and line up three and you have a long storage unit, E. Stack three lacquered cubes for a tall storage shelf unit with space on top for a record player, F. Courtesy Kemp Furniture.

Built-in practicality belongs in rooms where there's constant tracking back and forth, because it saves time, effort and, in the long run, money. In the garden room, *opposite and above*, the ceramic tile floor and prefinished plywood walls need only to be mopped or wiped. Painted, laminated plastic and oiled wood finishes and tops on furniture and washable slipcovers on wicker sofa and chair all wear well. Room designed by Carl Steele of Kunzig & Steele.

when practicality pays off

One of the hidden costs in decorating is the often overlooked cost of repair and replacement. Living takes its toll. After just a few years, fabrics fray, painted or papered walls show marks and dirt, carpets get worn and wood tabletops have burns, scratches and rings.

If you have a family or are moving into your own house or apartment, there's a good case to be made for investing in manmade materials with built-in endurance. Tough, easy-upkeep vinyls, laminated plastics, ceramic tile, and prefinished paneling make good sense in bathrooms, kitchens, family rooms, children's rooms, rooms opening onto the garden, where there is constant traffic and use. Plastic finishes also render vulnerable materials more resistant. You can protect a wood floor with a clear polyurethane varnish with a high shine or a matt finish and treat wood walls with a similar coating. Should you prefer to paint the floor, an epoxy paint stands up best. Vinyl wallcoverings, while more expensive than paper as a general rule, can be cleaned and are practical for surfaces other than walls, too.

On the other hand, you can economize by using inexpensive washable cotton and knit fabrics for slipcovers, curtains and bedspreads and by buying unfinished furniture and painting it yourself. Should the surface get burned or marred, all you have to do is sand it down and repaint. With other types of wood furniture, an oil or wax finish that can be rubbed down is preferable to a high finish that retains rings and marks.

When you make any major investment, such as carpeting a room, bear in mind the cost of upkeep and replacement. You may be better off buying carpet tiles, which can be removed should one section get worn or stained, rather than solid carpet. In cities, where grime comes in through the windows, shutters, washable shades or inexpensive washable ready-made sheers make more sense than heavy, costly lined curtains. Washable slipcovers are preferable to upholstery that needs professional cleaning, and while vinyl upholstery is good because you merely have to wipe it off, it is practical only up to a point. If you get a burn or hole in it, the sofa or chair will have to be recovered or, in some instances, replaced. The profit in practicality lies in knowing how to make it work for you.

A   B

THE VINYL TAKEOVER

Vinyl is in with the current generation who are more interested in carefree living than the shibboleths of decorating chic. There isn't a room in the house that can't benefit from the vinyl touch.

Dining area is saturated with the color and pattern of marigolds on a field of glossy black vinyl, A. The wallcovering, continued on a screen that hides corner pipes, is simple to hang and remove. Floor is tiled with vinyl in a quiet spatterdash design, and the plant ledge wears a coat of protective waterproof paint. Courtesy General Tire & Rubber Co.

Kitchen armored with vinyl and laminated plastic reduces clean-up to the minimum, B. Not only the walls and counter, but also the chair seats and backs, are vinyl-sheathed. Laminated plastic faces countertops, table; shutters and dado are prefinished plywood. Courtesy Sanitas.

Child's room revels in washable walls of a hand-printed vinyl mural designed like a crayon drawing to inspire a young artist, C. Soft-edge furnishings are great for play and easy upkeep: synthetic carpeting to cushion falls, bouncy lightweight foam cubes and mattresses slipcovered in washable stretch fabrics that take vigorous handling. Courtesy Wallcovering Industry Bureau.

Family room follows the trend toward a combination of shiny vinyl and high-gloss plastic paint, D. A panel of boldly printed vinyl hangs like an abstract painting against walls covered with wet-look vinyl. Lightweight furniture can be switched around without fuss and without leaving marks on the floor, also vinyl. Courtesy Wallcovering Industry Bureau.

Living room glories in furniture with fashionably curving contours upholstered in inexpensive vinyl that cleans off with a damp sponge, E. A durable cotton print covers the sofa cushions. Floor is vinyl tile and walls are paneled with pecky cypress finish plywood. Courtesy Syroco.

Dressing area is a quick remodeling job with vinyl and plastic, F. A sheet of light-filtering translucent plastic takes the place of a window (a good stratagem for updating a bad window in the bedroom of an old house and increasing privacy) and vinyl covers walls and floors. Laminated plastic top on desk forms a long dressing-table counter. Courtesy Sanitas.

C

D

E

F

Vinyl look-alikes for traditional materials and luxury fabrics are not only more practical and frequently less costly than the real thing, but also much simpler to cope with, which endears them to the do-it-yourself band.

Grasscloth vinyl has the virtues of being stain-resistant and washable, which makes it an eminently desirable material for a dining room or kitchen. In the space-shy dining area, *below,* the vinyl wall covering is carried over a simple built-in shelf which serves as a buffet for dinner parties.
Moire-patterned vinyl combines practicality with a look of utter luxury for a powder room or a dressing and make-up area lopped off one end of a bedroom, *opposite*. The pattern covers the walls, the shelf that acts as a dressing table, the inside of the door, and is looped into a window shade.
Cherry-planking vinyl, so realistic you have to touch it to know what it is made of, represents an easy way to get the look of a Colonial interior, *opposite bottom,* and is much simpler than covering walls and screens with plywood panels that have to be cut to size. All courtesy General Tire & Rubber Co.

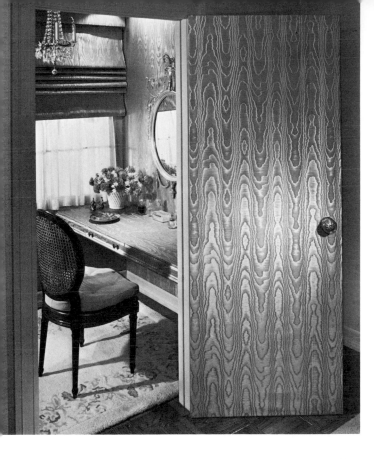

The decorating profit motive lies in furnishings that don't have to be replaced, repainted or prematurely retired. Laminated plastics, while calling for a sizable outlay of cash, pay off in the long run because they are easy to install (you can buy them precut to fit your specifications), easy to care for and practically indestructible unless you are a domestic firebug. Kitchens, bathrooms, family rooms, basements—any places that get hard and constant use—are candidates for plastic improvements.

Working wall built across one end of a family room, *below,* is a handsome assemblage of laminated plastics in two finishes, one plain, one tortoiseshell, on made-to-order sections—cabinets for stereo, storage and bar; shelves for books and accessories; countertop for desk or buffet. Cove lighting is recessed over side-wall niches. Room designed by Carl Steele of Kunzig & Steele.
Countrified kitchen with surfaces slick enough for grimy city living has walls and cabinets faced with woodgrain plastic, base cabinets and countertops in solid colors, a floor of vinyl brick roll goods, *opposite.* High ceiling of city apartment was dropped by building fake skylight, filling in soffit with plywood. Growth-promoting lights keep plants healthy in built-in niche. Designed by Joan Lerrick. Courtesy Formica.

spend to save

Bargain hunting, improvising and making do can go just so far in decorating an apartment or house. There's a good reason for splurging on some absolutely marvelous thing you would love to own, be it an oriental rug, a super storage system, an antique or a modern painting, because the sheer eye-catching quality of one outstanding object can make a room look infinitely better than the sum of its parts. If you are working within a budget, don't be haphazard. Figure out how much you can set aside for the major purchase around which you will build your room scheme and spend the rest for well-designed but inexpensive furnishings that will not compete with or distract from it.

Save your decorative superlative for the rooms that will be seen the most—the living or dining rooms—or the place it will give you the most pleasure. Don't, however, put a lot of cash into something large or permanent if you don't know where your next move is going to be. If you can't take it with you, or if it will be too big to fit in, that's just money wasted. In this case, you are better off collecting works of art or small decorative objects of a single persuasion—art glass, china, apothecary jars, silver. Modern reproductions of antique china such as Creil are less costly, but look almost as good as originals.

If you are lucky, you may own or inherit a superb antique, such as an armoire or breakfront, which can be converted for today's purposes into a bar, stereo or china closet. Or, if you are creative and clever with your hands, you can take a well-proportioned but drab secondhand wood table or chest and either paint on a fantasy finish such as marble or malachite or cover it with découpage. To buy such a piece would cost a mint, but if you have the time and enthusiasm for this kind of project you can achieve something personal, lasting and eminently satisfying—because it's all your own work.

A unique piece of furniture, so beautiful and arresting that it makes the most nondescript room seem impressive, is a worthwhile investment. One example: the Fornasetti secretary, *opposite,* a delicate fantasy of trompe l'oeil architecture in black, white and gray tones, a standout against a white wall (to which you might add wood, rag stock or painted moldings which make a boxy room look better proportioned). A less expensive alternate would be a Hong Kong reproduction of a lacquered Queen Anne secretary. Room designed by George Headly.

A

B

C

D

A complete storage wall system costing almost $2,000 may sound like wild extravagance, but not when you consider it as a lifetime investment. In a one-room apartment, *A*, a series of modular units with off-white lacquer finish, 88 inches high, eliminates the need for many separate pieces of furniture. In one space-saving wall, you have specialized storage for table linens, flatware, clothes, music, books, plus a built-in bar, a desk with a safe and two lighted display shelves. Should you move, the free-standing units can be used separately in different rooms of your next home or apartment. Furniture by Flair, Inc.

A beautiful marble table is a rather weighty proposition, but one of marbleized wood is just as handsome and twice as practical. It would pay you to have a Victorian table painted in a workshop, if you don't have the skill. The table and a reproduction chandelier form the focus of a small but stylish dining area, *B*. The chairs are inexpensive, the walls a simple home carpentry project consisting of thin wood strips nailed to a frame like a lattice. Room designed by Reg Adams.

A modern Chinoiserie breakfront from Italy is the kind of really impressive overscaled piece of furniture that adds dimension and drama to a small living room, *C*, where the rest of the furniture is light in scale. Beautiful and timeless in design, it is just as much at home in a modern as in a traditional setting. Room designed by Audrey Fellows, A.I.D. Courtesy Du Pont.

Handmade rugs and hangings, arrestingly graphic in design and color, are not only fun to collect, but when massed on a wall make an unusual alternative to the familiar art grouping, *D*. In an apartment where the furniture is clean-lined and classic in the modern idiom, the warmth and texture of contemporary crafts like this are especially welcome. Courtesy Regal Rugs.

Art is your first resort when you want to pull off a major decorative effect without spending too much time, effort, or even money, for nowadays there are budget-oriented museum lending services and a national mail-order company that sells medium-priced original paintings and graphics. It's up to you, though, to be your own display artist. You might hang a huge painting or a mass of smaller ones on one wall, spread your treasures around on panels of color or suspend a large abstract canvas within a frame as a room divider. A light or kinetic sculpture might be the solitary accessory on a coffee table, or a sculpture, spotlighted from above, the focal point in an entrance.

Contemporary graphics and a chrome sculpture shaped like a giant hub cap turn a featureless entrance hall leading to a living room into a small-scale version of a gallery, *above*. The sole piece of furniture is a museum-style bench. End wall and plywood panel painted in vibrant primary colors set off the sculpture and a series of small related prints. Designed by John Elmo, A.I.D.

Small oils and drawings of eighteenth and nineteenth century vintage, interspersed with wood carvings and architectural details, look more impressive when grouped in symmetrical balance, *opposite top*, than when dissipated around the room. To avoid mistakes, block out the grouping on the floor or a sheet of paper before hanging. Designed by Jerome Manashaw, A.I.D. Courtesy Du Pont.

African art requires a background that will throw the intriguing primitive shapes into relief. False wall of rough textured boards in the corner of a living room, *opposite bottom*, creates niches toward which the conversation group is oriented. Room designed by Allen Scruggs for State Pavilion.

Collections of china, glass, memorabilia, or whatever happens to be your particular passion can be exploited for their esthetic as well as their intrinsic value. The trick is massing them in one area, where they can make a strong decorative statement, rather than scattering them hither and yon.

Oriental porcelains take center stage in a small dining room, *opposite top.* Instead of buying an expensive, bulky cabinet, an archway was closed in, lined with adjustable shelves backed by pale celadon watered-silk vinyl. Ceiling spots illuminate shelves. Room designed by Wilds & Cannon.
Crystal bibelots, from paperweights to candlesticks, can be admired at conversational level when assembled on a glass-topped coffee table, *opposite bottom.* Table tops are excellent display points for small objects that need to be viewed in the round. Room designed by Reg Adams.
Mercury glass and chrome, concentrated around a sofa on end and coffee tables, *above,* lighten a dark-neutral scheme of brown, black and white with the sparkle of their highly reflective surfaces. Room designed by Allen Scruggs. Courtesy Window Shade Manufacturers Assn.

Money spent on a beautiful background is money well spent, for one broad and glorious sweep of an utterly luxurious material can go a long way toward making a room look better than it actually is.

Marble tile floor, although expensive, is indestructible, lasts forever, and brings a note of sheer elegance to a starkly furnished modern dining room, *A*. (Such permanent installations are advisable only if you own your house or apartment.) Room designed by Louis Bromante, N.S.I.D.
Vinyl tile floor with a big bold pattern and a striped border is comparable in appearance and price to wall-to-wall carpeting, but more practical for rooms that get heavy traffic, *B*. When you put this much pattern on the floor, make sure it's a design you can live with. Designed by Jerry Jerrard, N.S.I.D., for Amtico.
An oriental rug is worth spending money on because it lasts, mellows with age and, while perfect with antiques or reproductions, also makes inexpensive modern furniture seem better by association, *C*. Geometrics, which combine well with other patterns in a room, are good choices. Small rugs, which can fit any area, are better buys than huge ones. For bargains in orientals, seek out cleaners who hold sales of unclaimed rugs. Room designed by Sue Morris. Courtesy Window Shade Manufacturers Assn.
Silver vinyl wallcoverings in two patterns with oriental derivations—hawthorn boughs and bamboo fret—are a permissible indulgence in a dining room with simple, inexpensive furniture, *D*, because of their razzle-dazzle decorative quality. Room designed by Ron Budny, N.S.I.D., for Lloyd Wallcoverings.

A

B

C

D

more ideas than money

When you are decorating on a limited amount of money, imagination can be your substitute for a healthy bank account. Should you be short on ideas as well, look at what the experts have done. Study American and foreign decorating and home magazines (some of the brightest solutions to universal living problems seem to be hatched in Europe and Scandinavia), books that show the work of today's talented interior designers, and the model rooms put together by department stores. Once you have a general picture of what you would like in fabrics, furniture and accessories, a few days' scouting can save you a lot of cash. You should always shop around and compare prices, because we live in a fiercely competitive marketplace where any innovation in design reaches the mass level in a relatively short time, often in a copy of the original "knocked off" in countries where labor costs are low. Even dime stores now carry quite acceptable home furnishings (though not for a dime), and if you

Two versions of the same room demonstrate how the appearance can be completely altered by nothing more than a change of accent colors, accessories and a few pieces of furniture while the basic background of neutrals remains the same. In each case, the wallcovering of striped polyester and cotton, which also helps to blend the sleep sofas with the walls, and the carpeting are unchanged. With no major make-over and very little effort, a romantic and traditional mood, *opposite,* is exchanged for a crisp, contemporary one, *above.* Designed by Lee Bailey for Eastman Chemical.

can't find anything that sends you in your home town, write for catalogues of the mail-order companies that advertise in national home-furnishings magazines and newspapers and to Sears Roebuck, a huge company that within the last few years has branched out considerably in the furnishings field, hiring top designers and merchandising their designs all across the country.

While it certainly helps to be handy enough to take on simple remodeling and building projects, it is often smarter (and undoubtedly easier) to disguise architectural defects like bad walls, too-high ceilings, off-center windows and projecting pipes with fabrics, wallcoverings and screens than to make major structural changes.

You'll find it pays to be inventive with inexpensive fabrics like printed cottons, drip-dry sheets, dress goods and Indian printed bedspreads which can give you a big effect for very little money.

TODAY'S SHEETS COVER MORE THAN BEDS

Now that sheets are being styled by top designers in a great range of colors and patterns, they have become the hottest—or coolest—item in town for do-it-yourself decorating. (Even actress Jane Russell did over her apartment in sheets.) These new sheets, mostly permanent press, which means they keep their shape and crispness and drip dry, can often be snapped up in odd lots at white sales. Look for the flat double-, queen- or king-size which are the most practical buys.

Basket-weave sheets designed by Bill Blass, *opposite,* were the inspiration for a color scheme in the same natural tones and woven textures with the sheets applied to the wall as dado, bedhead panel and corner "screen." Note the tatami matting shades and the decorative trick of mounting a trio of inexpensive reproduction plates over the windows. Room designed by Lee Bailey for Eastman Chemical.
Toile sheets and matching ready-made bedspread were a real money-saver in the traditional bedroom, *above,* which would have been much costlier if real toile fabric had been used. With this type of pattern, where you have to match a repeat, the extra width of sheets is an asset. Courtesy Burlington Industries.

Revamp an old bathroom, *above left,* with three queen-size sheets and watch everything come up roses, from the walls and lavatory counter (to which the sheets are attached with double-faced tape) to the shower curtain (reinforced with a plastic liner) and blind (iron the sheet to adhesive-backed shade cloth). Outline the window with glued-on rickrack braid. To carpet the small area, get the washable kind you buy in a kit and cut to size. For directions, see page 180. Courtesy Celanese.

Transform a bedroom, *above right,* with punchily patterned sheets that come in reverse patterns, dark for the top sheet, light for the bottom. Make Roman shades, bedspread and table skirt from king-size top sheets, glue the bottom sheet to a six-panel screen. Lay carpet tiles to give the effect of a room-size rug. Indoor planters can be contrived from window boxes painted white. Courtesy Sears.

Cover up imperfect walls, *opposite top,* by shirring king-size sheets on curtain rods, attaching them at ceiling and baseboard with hooks. The see-through lattice pattern makes the small bedroom seem more spacious, and the softly draped fabric gives a more furnished feeling. Carry out the garden ambiance with a floral spread and sheets. Courtesy Springs Mills, Inc.

Glamorize a guest room, *opposite bottom,* for very little money with pretty printed sheets lavished on the walls, bed and at the windows. If you're a good sewer, you could make an Austrian shade and scallop the border of the sheet for a room-circling valance, cover foam-rubber pads for the window seat and the back rests that make the bed comfortable enough for daytime seating. Glue the sheets to the walls and the front of the drawer below the window seat. Designed by James Childs Morse, A.I.D. Courtesy Window Shade Manufacturers Assn.

103

FABRIC TRANSFORMATIONS

The vogue for pattern that started a few years ago represents one of the surest ways to give rooms style. Nor need it be costly with so many well-designed, low-priced fabrics around.

Make a splash with paisley, specifically, the printed cotton bedspreads from India that can be bought anywhere at a reasonable $6 to $8. The design is ageless, equally right in modern or traditional settings. For a formal Louis XVI room, *above,* designer Barbara D'Arcy of Blooming-dale's lavished the spreads all over the background, utilizing the borders for valances, then repeated the pattern on a sofa, tub chair and accent pillows. In a contemporary room, you might use them for wall covering and window shades, combined with colorful painted and plastic furniture.

Pick a simple print with a small-scale motif running in regular stripes as the main decoration for a small guest room, *opposite top.* Glue the broader stripe to walls and ceiling as a border, pleat the fabric for a lamp shade. Shutters instead of curtains keep the space uncluttered. Designed by Joan Spiro.

Mix five easy patterns to give a small apartment the fashionable pattern-on-pattern look, *opposite center.* As the fabrics, from Sears, are 54 inches wide, you can do a lot with minimum yardage. Control the profusion of pattern by using color-coordinated florals and geometrics— cane motif on walls, large and small scale florals for sofa and chairs, giant plaid for table skirt, damask motif for curtains and shade (covers, shade and curtains can be made to order by Sears custom shop).

Remodel with fabric by hiding an old bathroom's blemishes with a printed cotton, *opposite bottom.* Tape the print to walls, glue it to the Parsons table turned vanity (for directions, see page 178) and the plywood-panel disguise for the window. An old mirror frame hung over the center cut-out, sheers behind, give a tintype effect. Designed by Roz Mallin, N.S.I.D., for Celanese.

Turn a tiny hallway leading to a bedroom into a quiet and cozy library and game area, *above*, with the unifying touch of a striped fabric glued to walls, bookshelves and small Parsons table, upholstered on chair seats and backs. Run the stripe horizontally to make the tall, narrow space seem wider. Designed by J. Neil Stevens of McMillen, Inc., for Celanese House.

Carry crewel, an inexpensive Indian cotton version, over the bed and padded headboard and up the wall to make this area the color and pattern point of the room, *opposite top;* cover the lounge chair and ottoman with the same fabric. Utilize the ceiling beam often found in modern buildings by installing behind it a panel of diffused light controlled by a dimmer. Room designed by Carl Steele of Kunzig & Steele.

Print a room scheme black and white with four different bold designs (five if you count the fake zebra rug), *opposite bottom*. With black and white, there is no problem about throwing this much pattern around a room, but it is advisable to slipcover, rather than upholster, the furniture, in case you want to change one or more of the fabrics. Designed by Martin Kuckly, N.S.I.D.

BEDS CAN BE BEAUTIFUL

Split a bedroom between two sisters with a separate-but-equal arrangement of pressure-pole systems that provides niches for the twin beds, night tables and toy storage, *above*. Make a mock half-canopy by continuing the bedspread fabric up the wall and onto the ceiling, gluing it firmly in place. Room designed by Emily Malino, A.I.D. Courtesy Window Shade Manufacturers Assn.
Move the bed out from the wall by putting the mattress on an inexpensive elevated platform base in the center of the room, *opposite top*. Dramatic overhead lighting which eliminates need for lamps and night tables is a square box of thin plywood suspended from ceiling beam with wires and screw-eyes. Down lights inside box are linked to outlet for old ceiling fixture, controlled by wall switch. Wicker baskets along wall are neat way to store out-of-season clothes. Designed by Terry Capuana.
Frame a bed with 3 x 3's for a sleek modern version of the old four-poster, *opposite bottom*. Cover frame and padded headboard with stretch fabric, attach a panel of the same fabric with Velcro to the wall between two windows (if it were a window wall, you could staple the fabric to a light-blocking panel). You can repeat the fabric on table, chair seats. Designed by Lee Bailey for Eastman Chemical.

WAYS TO SQUEEZE IN STORAGE

Lop three feet off the end of a room and you have enough space to build a compact work center for sewing or crafts, *above*. Take advantage of natural light with a drop-down sewing table (push it back against the pegboard wall after use, tuck away the folding chair, and a window seat emerges). Striped pull-down shades over closets, wood valance covered with the printed curtain fabric tie the unit in with the window treatment. Designed by Shirley Regendahl. Courtesy Window Shade Manufacturers Assn.

Cut across the corner of a small bedroom and gain a roomy closet, *opposite top*. Hinged wood panels, finished with painted moldings, serve as doors on two sides. In center, two panels slide like a screen on a track attached to the ceiling. Designed by David Barrett, A.I.D.

Improvise a laundry and storage area in a nursery with a simple wood built-in, *opposite center*. Pull-down shades screen shelves over painted chest, conceal clothes dryer. Front of washer is disguised with plywood strips; strap hinges match door treatment. Designed by Peg Walker. Courtesy Celanese.

Promote bigger and better parties by building a bar and serving counters across one end of a living room, *opposite bottom*, mirroring the alcoves to make the room seem longer. For unusual doors, frame pierced plywood panels and back them with rigid plastic. Designed by Tom Ashjean, A.I.D. Courtesy *Better Homes & Gardens*.

FIND YOURSELF A NICHE

The niche or alcove represents a centuries-old idea for providing indoor comfort and privacy that bears reviving. Modern space-shy apartments benefit from built-in niches where you can hide an unmade bed, stash your work-in-progress or simply curl up and luxuriate in a snug cocoon.

Camouflage the bed in a studio apartment with a sliding wall of screens hung from a ceiling track that can be pulled across one end of the room during the day, *opposite top.* You can put together the simple framework yourself and use sheets for the backing and to make a cover and pillow shams for the studio bed. Courtesy Burlington Industries.

Take over the bedroom closet and equip it as a private alcove for sewing or other hobbies, *opposite bottom.* Mirrors, needed for fittings, that line the inside of the bi-fold doors also make the small space seem less confined. To blend the doors into the bedroom wall, cover the outside with fabric that matches the wallpaper, shirring it on rods. For appearance's sake, you might also line the alcove with the same paper. Parsons tables of two heights, one designed to slide under the other, a simple chair, wall lights and a molded plastic catch-all for organizing sewing supplies are all that you need to make the tiny area an efficient workroom. Designed by Joe Minicucci. Courtesy Tyndale, Inc.

Tuck a TV and stereo hideaway under the eaves of an attic room, *below left.* Build a platform where you can nap or stretch out, shelves for record player, speakers, books, add knockdown paper-and-plastic stools as end tables, a rug and a chair. Designed by Peg Walker. Courtesy J. Josephson, Inc.

Construct a seating niche with a jigsaw structure of wood, *below right,* that combines shelves, coffee table and built-in lighting, and a platform padded with persimmon plush as a vantage point for a glass-walled living room. Hang transparent Fiberglas shades to insulate the glass by day, a second, room-darkening set to pull over them at night. Designed by Vladimir Kagan. Courtesy Window Shade Manufacturers Assn.

A

B

C

D   E

HOW TO FAKE IT

Fool-the-eye frauds that look like the real thing but aren't, decorative deceptions that have been around since the days of the Romans, are even quicker
and cheaper now, with our versatile materials.

Give an illusion of eating outdoors to a closed-in dining area, A. The latticework that encloses
the corner is the common garden type you buy in sections. Instead of a balloon mural, you
might have painted clouds or a scenic paper. Room designed by Leona Kahn, N.S.I.D.
Simulate a country air in a city living room with false beams, B, a fantastically realistic piece of
fakery that apes the mellow, hand-hewn look of old wood in molded plastic or plywood
(plywood beams cost just under $1 per running foot). Courtesy W & J Sloane.
Pitch a tent in a minuscule dining room and you'll feel you've been transported back to a more
elegant age, C. For the tent effect, drape the ceiling with fabric mitered to meet in the center,
anchor it to a hook in the middle and staple or tack it to wood strips along the walls. Cover
the walls with the same striped fabric and hide joins with a molding. Use matching tie-backs,
valance. For decoration, display porcelain figures on white-painted wall brackets. Room designed
by Jane Victor, N.S.I.D.
Brush up an apartment kitchen with painted *faux bois* on standard cabinets; add painted bamboo
moldings to cabinets and shutters, D. "Planking" floor is vinyl fake. Designed by Florence Hewitt.
"Tile" a plain fireplace with a design stenciled over the white-painted brick, E. The trick is to
space the pattern to cover every three bricks, utilizing the grout so it appears to come between
the tiles. You could do a kitchen wall the same way. Designed by Bishop & Lord.

A

B

C

D

DECORATIVE COVER-UPS FOR FLAWS

When rooms are less than architectural perfection, it pays to know how to disguise their unattractive features with some speedy sleight of hand.

Mask off-center windows with a false frame, built out to the second molding to leave space behind for sheer curtains, light strips, *A*. Room designed by Alfred Andriola.
Conceal corner pipes, the kind that carry steam heat in old apartments, with a folding screen, blended with the walls by the common bond of a washable vinyl covering, *B*. An unpainted Parsons table might be covered with the same vinyl. Courtesy Wallcovering Industry Bureau.
Lower a high ceiling, visually if not actually, by hanging a series of fabric panels like banners at various levels, *C;* add hanging lamps for low-down lighting. It's a neat way to brighten a cramped kitchen-cum-dining area. Designed by Donald Cameron for Celanese.
Hide a hideous fireplace with an avant-garde assemblage of plywood panels soaring to different heights and lit from behind, *D*. Designed by Donald Cameron for Celanese.

MAKING SPACE TO WORK AT HOME

However limited your living quarters, you can always fit in a desk and files if
you use your ingenuity.

Steal space in a bedroom, *opposite top,* for a small desk (which might double as a dressing table)
and a standard file cabinet papered to match the walls, as a retreat for writing letters, paying
bills. Room designed by Camille Lehman, A.I.D. Courtesy Window Shade Manufacturers Assn.
Annex the corner of a living room, *opposite bottom,* and build a simple wood counter over an
unpainted chest; add a wall-hung drawer unit and cover everything to match the walls in a
hard-wearing, unobtrusive vinyl facsimile of cork. Courtesy General Tire & Rubber Co.
Take over a closet that has a window, *above,* as your private study. All you need in the way of
furniture are file cabinets topped by a laminated plastic counter, chairs that give you good
support, and shelves for reference books. For decoration's sake, you might add a good-looking
window shade, a personal collection of folk art. Designed by Charles Kriebel. Courtesy Window
Shade Manufacturers Assn.

A

B

D

IF YOU'VE GOT IT, FLAUNT IT

A collection doesn't have to be expensive to be eye-worthy. Sometimes the most ordinary things, imaginatively displayed, can be more fun to look at than a cabinet full of cut crystal. All you need is a blank wall or empty shelves, a good sense of arrangement and the courage to be different.

Expose your cooking paraphernalia if you like to live and eat in the kitchen, A. It's not only appropriate, but it makes sense to put things where you can get at them easily. You might paint each section of the wall behind a storage unit a different tone of the red-orange family so the shapes and textures of objects such as a ravioli cutter, trivets, ceramic bowls and canisters are thrown into relief. Designed by Harry Schule and John McCarville. Courtesy Royal System.
Bring out all the baskets you've picked up here and there over the years and group them in a deliberately haphazard fashion on the wall of a dining room, B, which is more offbeat than a studied arrangement. If you have a collection of old-fashioned china, such as ironstone, a dresser or wall shelves make good display points. Designed by Louis Bromante, N.S.I.D.
Reveal the keys you've filched from hotels all over the world by hanging them boldly on pegboard, C, and you'll have an instant attraction for the curious visitor (keys from European hotels, incidentally, have the most decorative name tags). If not keys, any object of innocent kleptomania or collector's mania will do. Some people collect ashtrays, others, hats.
Pick out a few plates of different sizes from your everyday china (they should be decorative in shape or color like the inexpensive Japanese copy of the Meissen onion pattern, D), mount them on a wall painted a deep color. Room designed by Lee Bailey. Courtesy Eastman Chemical.

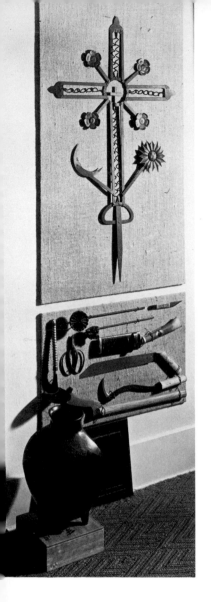

ONE WAY TO LIVE WITH A COLLECTION

A collection can become the theme of your decoration provided you collect something colorful, interesting, and meant to be lived with and enjoyed, like folk art. Instead of letting all those objects you picked up on your travels gather dust in a closet, emulate Ellen Sheridan, who originated what she calls "decorative storage" by arranging her treasures in designs on wall panels and, when she ran out of wall space, on the panels of doors. While you may not have as varied or complete a collection, you can adapt many of her ideas for displaying small figures and things that are hard to group.

Shelves across a window, *opposite right,* silhouette clay figures with fanciful shapes, mostly from Mexico. Hand-carved combs and bread molds hang in a striking design on the painted end panel of a storage unit.

Panels of hardboad covered with coarse natural linen are attached to the wall as a backdrop for the beautiful shapes of Japanese carpenters' and garden tools, held in place with pieces of wire, and a delicate metal sculpture, *opposite left.*

Door panels framed by wide old-fashioned trim are painted blue above, red below, a very simple way to show off the lines of wood carvings. *Below, left,* a San Blas Island witch doctor's figure, a primitive weaving. *Below right,* a carved wood crucifix, a wooden star. Broad strips of felt hung on wall of corridor make a striking backing for Mexican paintings.

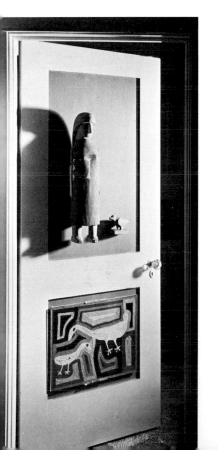

self-expression on a shoestring

To get a look that is yours and yours alone takes ingenuity and originality in today's mass-produced apartments and houses with their standardized architecture and cookie-cut living quarters, but there's no need to let it throw you. There are plenty of well-styled inexpensive home furnishings around and if the furniture or fabrics don't hold up forever—who needs it? You'll be moving on anyway, and as your tastes and needs change you'll either discard what you outgrow or find another use for it. What you need now is a home that suits your current living style and reflects you as a person—or a family.

Think in terms of expanding the space at your disposal visually and making it work for you. Keep clutter at a minimum, color schemes clear, clean and straightforward, patterns and colors limited; put pattern where it will count most—at the windows, on upholstered furniture, the walls or the floor, if you have low ceilings. Select multipurpose furniture in simple shapes and styles, area or room-size rugs you can fit into your next home, window treatments that are inexpensive, mobile lighting such as lamps and portable spotlights on a track (in some apartments you can't even put a fixture in the ceiling because it is poured concrete), sectional storage units.

Remember, too, that you will be expected to return a rental apartment to its original condition when you move; meanwhile you need the landlord's permission to paint or stain the floor, paint the walls a dark color or cover them up (however, the new strippable papers and fabric attached with Velcro tape are easy to remove). Wall-to-wall carpeting should be of a tackless installation and bathroom carpeting, carpet tiles or vinyl tiles put down with double-faced tape, not bonded to the floor. A little forethought now will save you future trouble and expense.

Casual nook by window, an improvisation for carefree low-level dining, *opposite top,* mingles stools, butcher-block table that tucks under plastic serving shelf and a swinging paper lantern, with floor purposely left bare. Mirrored panels held in channels and vertical plastic blinds visually widen the minimum space. Designed by Inman Cook, A.I.D. Courtesy Celanese.
Elegant corner near kitchen (hidden from view by a free-standing screen), *opposite bottom,* has all the elements of a formal dining room on a reduced scale: area-defining rug in a strong design, neutral colors, reproduction armchairs, gracefully skirted table, black-lacquered buffet table, plus a few well selected accessories. Designed by Leif Pedersen, N.S.I.D.

NEW APARTMENT FOR OLD

Can an elderly one-room apartment, the kind you can often rent quite cheaply in the unfashionable neighborhoods of a large city, become a pleasant, attractive and functional place to live? Faced with just such a challenge, *opposite bottom,* Paul Krauss, A.I.D., performed an expert and imaginative make-over. First he covered the beat-up floors throughout the apartment with white sheet vinyl flecked with black and gray, then screened out the peeling painted walls and depressing fire escape view with a grand sweep of sunny yellow-and-white textured plaid rayon that emphasized the one saving grace, high ceilings, and gave the room a light airiness. Opaque butter-yellow shades were added for light control. The mood of the decorating scheme, *opposite top,* contemporary with traditional overtones, was initiated by a pair of old English mahogany armchairs. These, in turn, influenced the style of the window treatment (long tie-back curtains on painted wood rods) and the sleep sofa, even the proportions of the homemade armoire—a simple wood cabinet with doors of painted perforated hardboard—that stores clothes. TV, stereo and books, *below right.* All the furnishings, including the rayon area rug, are simple, inexpensive and practical. Mr. Krauss cleverly capitalized on the existing pass-through between kitchen and living room, *below left,* by placing over it a wide shelf that extends into both areas and serves as a dining table for four, two to a side, and also, since it is higher than a regulation table, a bar and kitchen work counter. A Roman shade of the plaid fabric can be lowered to hide the kitchen and blend the pass-through into the background. Miraculously, every element needed for comfortable living has been worked into the 12-by-18-foot space with remarkably little expenditure and no architectural remodeling. Courtesy Simmons.

Start from scratch in a first apartment with a simple, punchy modern scheme of black and white with accents of yellow and orange. Living-dining room, *opposite top,* gets a yellow cotton shag rug, white matchstick bamboo blind, and for seating twin white vinyl sofas on casters arranged at right angles with a yellow-painted end table between, an inflatable chair and cube coffee tables. Folding chairs with white frames, cane seats and an erector-kit black metal table, top painted yellow, take care of dining needs. Shelves of black metal bookcase, also made with kit, are painted to match the table. Inexpensive extras: white lamps by Progress, black-and-white super-graphic on white wall. In the bedroom, *opposite bottom,* a giant geometric black-and-white rug takes over the floor, drawing attention away from the king-size Simmons sleeper covered with a yellow-and-orange print. In another space-saving right-angle arrangement, white lacquered campaign chests line up with the bed and substitute for tables. A second, smaller rug, hung like a painting, repeats the bold geometric pattern on the floor. Huge puffy pillows switch from bed to floor for TV watching. Tiny hallway, *above,* with wicker storage hampers, secondhand Victorian mirror and hat rack, globe lights and photographs hung on Velcro strips is lighthearted and imaginative treatment of what might have been a dark, cluttered, catch-all space. Designed by Arlene Petroff. Courtesy Simmons.

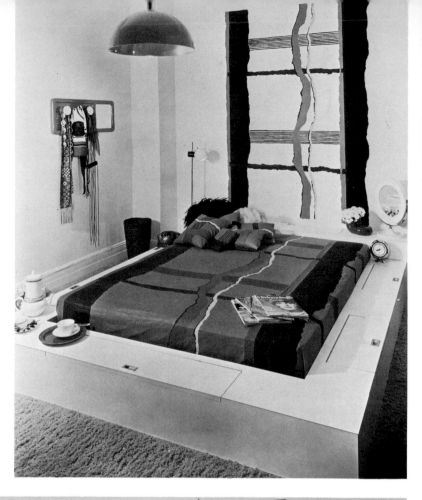

You don't have to redo an apartment completely to bring it up to date. Some-times all it takes is the replacement of a couple of pieces of outmoded or shabby cumbersome old furniture with something sleeker and chic-er, and a stimulating splash of different colors and patterns.

Retire old-fashioned furniture from your bedroom, *above,* and make yourself a swinging pad of a bed unit with sections that can be put together in a frame to perform all the functions of chests, night tables and what-have-you, *opposite top.* Play up the all important bed with a cover of abstract patterned fabric in zingy colors; run the same fabric, in reverse, in a panel up the wall. Spotlight the center of attraction with a simple modern floor lamp and hanging fixture. Should you feel like getting rid of the old rug too, you might replace it with carpet strips between bed and walls.

Switch a heavy sleep sofa of thirties vintage for a new sleek foam and-stretch-fabric model, *below* and *opposite bottom,* and you're halfway toward giving your apartment a fashionably eclectic look. Now you can be more enterprising with color and pattern, re-covering a dreary easy chair with a bright crewel fabric (add a footstool if you like), treating yourself to a new wing chair in a bold stripe, and changing the existing oriental rug for a smaller one with a stronger design. Add a modern lamp and some graphics mixed in with the family portraits and photographs and the room, while still retaining a traditional charm, becomes refreshingly livable. Courtesy Simmons.

SOLVING THE STUDIO SLEEPING PROBLEM

Select a sleep sofa to suit the style of your apartment from the new designs that marry comfort to good looks. A sofa upholstered in a stunning suedelike synthetic in bush-jacket beige with safari-style buckled arms over clear plastic panels, *above*, initiates the studio apartment color scheme of neutrals with orange accents. Black-and-white stripe of the room-darkening shades is picked up in the sheets, orange wall strips of cord-concealing felt by a tangerine blanket, *below*. Furniture of tubular metal or clear and colored plastic is easy to shift around, keeps floor space uncluttered. Designed by Peg Walker. Courtesy Window Shade Manufacturers Assn.
Save space with a swingaway bed that tucks into a wall of do-it-yourself plank paneling during the day, *opposite top*. Take advantage of the depth of the bed niche to build in a mini-bar and TV-music center alongside. Large painting should be firmly fixed to wall so it won't shift when the bed drops. When the bed wall opens, hinged bifold doors swing back to reveal stand-ins for night tables, plastic shelves with pin-up lamps above, *opposite bottom*. Print used to cover doors and niche and make curtains and pillow covers is color-coordinated to bright red carpeting. Designed by Lee Bailey for Eastman Chemical.

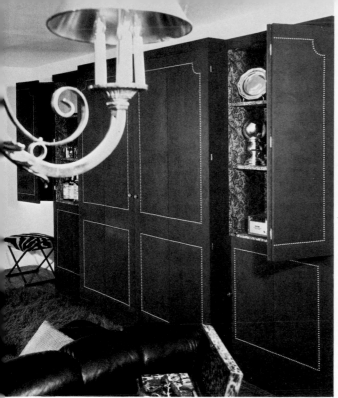

A

C

STORAGE YOU CAN TAKE WITH YOU

While there is almost no apartment, old or new, that has enough storage for all your belongings, remember that anything you build into a rental apartment must be removed when you leave and the walls repaired. You are better off buying or building units you can move like furniture.

Construct a storage unit with three sections, two for entertaining gear, the center to hold clothes or a murphy bed. The plainest wood can be improved with a facing of suedecloth studded with nailheads, A, and a lining of colorful paisley-patterned paper. Designed by Joan Spiro.
Improvise an armoire to hold all your linens by buying or making a wood cabinet, adding ball feet, finial and spiral twist moldings (from a building supply store) and a pediment cut from plywood, B. Cover shelves, insides of doors and boxes with a flowered vinyl that matches the walls. Courtesy Wallcovering Industry Bureau.
Put your money in furniture with built-in storage, like the campaign bed with three roomy drawers, C, and a matching shelf and drawer étagère. Such dual-purpose pieces can go into a future guest room or family room when you move. Courtesy Du Pont-Bernhardt Furniture.
Group sectional storage around a corner, instead of putting the sofas there, D. By moving the sofas away from the walls you get more use out of the space at your disposal. Inexpensive white-lacquered storage units like these are good buys because they can be split up and used alone or in many different combinations in any room. Courtesy Du Pont-Charlton Furniture.

D

THE STRATEGY OF SEATING

The seating arrangement in a living room is your first objective, as it will determine where you put the rest of the furniture. When you place your sofas and chairs, remember that no matter how large or small the room, a conversation group should have a focal point.

Take over a wall shelf with a symmetrical composition of a large dominant abstract painting flanked by stereo speakers (the cases painted white); square off sectional seating units in front, letting the well-finished backs of three units serve as a low room divider, *opposite top*. Repeat the upholstery colors in ready-made curtains, hung in panels, and three plastic hexagons bunched for a coffee table. Room designed by Delphene Richards, N.S.I.D. Courtesy *Family Circle.*

Fake a window of white plastic panels, "leaded" with liquid solder and lit from behind, as the main attraction for a pair of loveseats (quite simply, cushions on painted wood platforms), *opposite bottom*. Wide shelf padded with pillows beneath "window" and plastic swivel dining chairs round out the group. At a pinch (or a party) carpeted steps leading to the library level can also be perched on. Room designed by Emily Malino, A.I.D. Courtesy *Family Circle.*

Devise a gallery in miniature with galvanized metal panels fastened to wood strips at ceiling and floor levels, paintings hung by invisible nylon cords from hooks clipped on the top, *above left*. Spotlights on ceiling track pick out the art. To give the effect of a room within a room, one loveseat is backed with a pair of paintings hung like a room divider on nylon cords anchored to the floor, the other with sliding fabric panels on window tracks. Designed by Jane Victor, N.S.I.D.

Capitalize on a corner with a terrace view as the nucleus of a compact group of sectional seating units, pull-up chairs and stools that takes up minimum floor space in a small studio apartment, *above right*. See-through casement fabric stretched on wood shutter frames filters sunlight without getting in the way of the seating group. Designed by Lee Bailey for Eastman Chemical.

A

B

C

ROOM DIVIDERS THAT REDESIGN SPACE

The versatile, invaluable room divider plays many parts in the open plan. It can be a storage or display unit, the boundary between two areas with different functions within a single room, or a reshaper of floor space. With precut lumber, you can fashion a divider to suit your needs.

Replace the railing at the top of a stairwell with an open-shelf divider of white-painted wood, A, to create display space for plants, art and accessories. An alternate, should you need more storage space, would be a long low bank of closed cabinets.

Mark the boundary of a small, low-ceilinged entrance hall with a simple framework of vertical 3 x 3's and horizontal 1 x 3's, the latter forming open-core boxes that can be topped with panels of Carrara glass to show off plants, a shell collection, B. The linear structure, which repeats the vertical stripe of the papered wall, defines the limited area without closing it in claustrophobically. Designed by Hamilton-Howe.

Frame a dining area with a giant square that looks like a picture window without the glass, C. Here it draws the line between the living room and a small front porch that has been enclosed for dining. Designed by Robert Braunschweiger.

Set off an open-plan living room from the entrance with an airy partition of 2 x 5's, lacquered white, D, to give a feeling of visual separation without cutting off the light or interrupting the flow of space. Designed by Muller-Bachich.

D

THE ROLE OF THE RUG

While rugs and carpets are considered standard equipment for most apartment dwellers because of their sound-absorbing qualities, you should look on a rug as more than just a covering for the bare floor. The shape, size and design can both define and decorate the area it occupies.

Top wall-to-wall carpet with a large round rug to establish a sphere of interest for the conversation group in an L-shaped room, *opposite*. Inflatable chair and plastic coffee table can be placed on the rug without obscuring the design. This trick also works if the carpet came with the apartment and you want pattern and color on the floor. Courtesy Cabin Crafts-West Point Pepperell.

Let a textured rug mark off the dividing line between seating and dining areas of a small living room. Two-tone shag rug in soft greens is a good foil and a unifying background for the simple, lightly scaled Scandinavian teak furniture, *above*. Courtesy Du Pont.

Run a striped rug down the center of a one-room apartment as visual separation between modern Italian fiberglass sofa and chairs, white-painted chests with black trim, Victorian dining chairs and table, *below*. Horizontal super-stripe makes a narrow room look wider. Room designed by Jean Elliott. Courtesy Du Pont.

TALK ABOUT SUPER SEATING!

The contemporary way to handle a living room is to provide a clutch of cushiony, sprawly seating and very little else in the way of furniture. It's all part of our gregarious life style and just about the simplest way to have a room that's always turned on for a party.

Stretch a seating platform made from plywood along the window wall (where as a rule you wouldn't have much furniture) and let the soft shag carpeting roll right over it, *opposite top*. Pad the top with outsize floor cushions you can make yourself, toss lots of fur and fabric pillows along the back, and that's all there is to it. If you keep everything low down like this, even the lamps and paintings, you'll find a room with an 8-foot ceiling will seem much higher. Courtesy Du Pont.

Round up a string of sectional sofas in a mammoth semicircle where masses of people can sit at ease, *opposite bottom*. While this represents a sizable chunk of money, the effect is so opulent that you need very little else in the room—an extra chair or two, cube coffee tables or plastic-and-paper stools and a profusion of plants for living color. Courtesy Heritage Furniture.

Multiply your seating by pitching it at different levels in a series of steps, *below*. It's the seventies extension of the old non-furniture conversation pit. As this is something you build from plywood and cover with shag carpeting, it's a project to be undertaken only in a place you own or have on a long lease. Walls of the pit itself are topped with a border of stick-on walnut woodgrain tiles and a wet-look plastic runner for an easy-clean serving surface. You might paint a wall graphic in a color and pattern repeat of the carpet. Courtesy Sears.

TO GAIN SPACE, TURN THE CORNER

Follow the contours of three short walls with an S-bend of sectional sofas, *opposite top,* and triumph over the room's architectural problems. The combination: two corner units, three armless middle units and one bumper. Room designed by Richard Ryan of Bloomingdale's.
Corner a bed, back it with bolsters and let it double as seating pad, *opposite center.* Queen-size mattress on plywood frame, bolsters and Parsons table share sheets as a covering. Decorative directional signals: vinyl rickrack braid glued to walls, arrowheads cut from 12-inch-square blue vinyl tiles inset in solid white vinyl tile floor. Courtesy Burlington Industries.
Steer wall-hung units around a corner to provide storage for linens and china, books and music in living and dining areas of an L-shaped room, *opposite bottom.* Off-the-floor cabinets look less heavy in a small apartment. Room designed by Edmund Motyka, A.I.D. Courtesy Royal System.
Construct a series of niches with 2 x 4's for display and storage space in a one-room apartment, back them with three bright vinyls, picking up one pattern on the coffee tables, *below.*
Space-maker: Parsons table a bed can slide under. Room designed by Shirley Regendahl. Courtesy J. Josephson, Inc.

PROFIT FROM COLOR POWER

Strong color is the quickest attention-getter in decoration, a sure-fire way to direct the eye to whatever you want seen. Even a painting or a piece of sculpture stands out better against a background of color than against a plain white wall. If, for instance, you had a hallway or room with a superfluity of doors, you could turn them into assets by painting each one a different color and hanging objects against them, as Ellen Sheridan did with folk art (page 123).

Draw attention to paintings and sculpture with backgrounds in the yellow-orange family. In a dark inner hallway, *opposite,* this has the additional advantage of introducing warmth and brightness and giving the architecture continuity. When you make a bold color statement like this, keep other elements non-competitive. Here, almost everything is white, wood-toned or neutral, except for the flame-stitch pattern on stair treads and stool, a subdued combination of all the colors in the decoration. Designed by Carl Steele of Kunzig & Steele.
Play up a grand piano by bringing it out into the open (better acoustically than tucking it away in a corner) on a platform covered with sound-absorbing blue carpet, *below.* Cover the wall behind it with carpet in another primary—red. Designed by Paul Lester Weiner and Ala Damaz.

when does it pay
to remodel?

If you're an apartment dweller, the determining factors in a decision to remodel are the rent, the condition of the apartment, and the way you feel about it. Should you be lucky enough to find a low-rent apartment you love and look forward to living in as long as possible, it's worth spending some money getting it into shape. If this involves structural changes, show your landlord the plans (you'll have to get his permission), and should he feel you'll be improving his property he may even give you an allowance toward the costs. When you own your apartment, it's certainly worthwhile to fix it up, but don't put in more than you can reasonably expect to get back if you sell later.

The same rules apply to a house. Put money into remodeling your own place, but not more than you can recover. Buy the best equipment you can afford for bathrom and kitchen renovations. Big retail stores like Sears and discount stores have very good buys on equipment and can often supply the labor to install it. If you need a second bathroom, try to take advantage of existing water pipes and drains by backing the second up against the first.

Most remodeling is done for gain—of space, storage or bigger and better living areas—and you'll save by doing as much work yourself as you can. Architectural changes are the most complicated, so figure out ways to get around them. For instance, take windowless basements and sloping-walled attics, often regarded as dead space that can't be made livable without complete remodeling. Not so. With little more than bold color and pattern you can make them not only fit but fun to live in and fashion a room like no other.

Basement gets groovy when the walls and floor are painted first white, then with super-graphic designs as a setting for way-out furniture in hot orange plastic and purple plush, *opposite top*. "Rear window" consists of overlapping circles of wood at different depths framing trompe l'oeil vista of floating clouds, blue sky. Designed by Barbara D'Arcy of Bloomingdale's.
Attic turns apartment with the addition of a studio window, *opposite bottom*. Vinyl shades pull up from the bottom to control light. Wide-awake color is the keynote from red carpet and painted and stenciled furniture to the walls, a plywood facing over beams, lacquered shiny red. Courtesy Lord & Taylor.

A

B

C

REMODELING WITH COLOR AND PATTERN

Reshape the contours of a living room that is long and narrow, *A,* by painting the ceiling and carpeting the floor dark brown, *above.* Deep color above and below makes the room look squarer. To give it width, the sleep sofa, re-covered in a geometric print, is positioned against the windows rather than the wall and backed by a pair of narrow Parsons lamp tables. Tubular metal chairs and table and geometric rug round out the conversation group. Lower pair of shutters are painted white, top pair replaced by fabric shades matched to the sofa cover. Further revamping is mainly a matter of moving furniture—the piano to the wall niche (now lined with shelves for an African art collection), the chest opposite to balance its bulk. The only bright color in the brown, black and white scheme is introduced by a single dominant painting. Room designed by Arthur Leaman, A.I.D.

Release a small kitchen from its confines with trompe l'oeil fantasy on bland white cabinets, *C.* Cabinet at left combines blue-and-white *faux marbre,* kitchen-shelf découpage of objects snipped from magazines and ads. Serving alcove cabinets now sport bright blue painted moldings to match the painted trim of the door. Pattern on ceiling, a canopy of vinyl strips, and a tile facing in the alcove substitute for old pattern on the walls, *B.* New work and dining counter of blue laminated plastic fills in for old base cabinet. In switch of old-to-new equipment, refrigerator takes over the wall niche; ovens and cook top move to wall by door to dining room. Designed by Max Eckert.

A

B

Divide a long narrow kitchen, the type you find in the basement of a brownstone, into a dining area and cooking alcove, *A,* by building a short wall between, continuing it in a sculptural curve over the cooking area, *B.* Long dining area wall, stripped to bare brick and painted white, is doubled by reflection in mirrored short wall. Sober setup of metal kitchen cabinets and equipment is saved by a shiny foil paper that zaps the whole thing. Designed by Joan Spiro.
Remove the wall between an old-fashioned apartment kitchen and pantry to gain a compact dining and storage area, *E.* Wall behind dining counter is faced with mock brick similar to the brick vinyl flooring, opposite wall flushed out over stock cabinets to make them seem built in. Stock cabinets, painted a soft and mellow green, are used throughout; the splash panels in the kitchen, *C* and *D,* are covered with vinyl Delft tile. Designed by Robert Purdom.

C

D

ARCHITECTURE REVISED WITH PLYWOOD

If you want to change the background of a room completely, one of the most inexpensive of all the architectural remodeling materials is plywood paneling which adds the warmth of wood at a fraction of the cost of the real thing. Though large, the panels are light enough to install yourself.

Take a typical apartment living room, circa 1930, with nothing much in its favor except the beamed ceiling, *opposite top,* and after a make-over with plywood paneling you'd never recognize it, despite the fact that much of the furniture and its placement remain the same. The entrance wall, *above,* was remodeled to eliminate an old-fashioned fireplace (replaced by a facing of sleek, contemporary black slate); the arched entrance and a book niche are now enclosed behind a door and used for storage. The opposite wall was also furred out and paneled and turned into a floor-to-ceiling book and art display wall, with shelves and oversized shadow boxes lined with gold suede cloth and illuminated by light troughs hidden behind paneled strips, *opposite bottom.* Despite the fact that the room has less wall space than before, the unifying effect of the paneling and new wall-to-wall carpeting actually makes it seem much larger. Designed by Virginia Frankel. Courtesy U.S. Plywood.

A

B

C

ROOM FOR IMPROVEMENT

There's almost no room that can't be changed for the better. Sometimes the simplest remodeling job is all it takes to add an entirely new dimension.

Update an old porch by filling it in with insulated glass and installing heat and you have an extra living room that's a real sun trap, A. Vertical blinds (in the same white as the woodwork) that rotate 180 degrees give plants and people just the amount of light they like. Increase your planting with hanging baskets suspended from the ceiling. For color accents, cushion wicker and rattan porch furniture, Mexican children's chairs in luscious ice-cream tints—orange, raspberry, strawberry, lemon, lime-mint and candied violet; use patterned synthetic carpeting in hot pink and orange. Room designed by Camille Lehman, A.I.D. Courtesy Window Shade Manufacturers Assn.

Get more use from a dining room by furring out one wall to a depth that will hold a murphy bed for a guest, B, covering it with handsome rosewood plywood panels, C. Panel the door to the kitchen and a second door to a small guest bath or powder room so that when they are closed the wall looks as if it is solid wood. Alternate idea would be to build a storage wall for linens, silver and wine. Designed by Albert Herbert, A.I.D. Courtesy U.S. Plywood.

Re-form a fireplace in a dining room to gain seating and serving space for parties, D. Disguise the chimney breast with a panel of white-lacquered plywood and replace the old low hearth with a long raised shelf that, suitably padded, becomes a banquette for seated dinners with the addition of a slim Parsons table or tray tables. Should you want to keep the fireplace working, use fire-resistant material under the chimney area. Designed by Barbara D'Arcy of Bloomingdale's.

D

OLD BATHROOMS REGENERATED

Revive a bathroom that's functional but on the clinical side with the shot-in-the-arm color of a vivid daisy-patterned vinyl, *opposite*. In a real switch, put it on the ceiling, floor, countertop and backsplash, at the windows—everywhere but on the walls. Cut out daisies and glue them on drawer fronts, around knobs (remove these first, replace afterward) and on the wall. Lacquer window frames, the old medicine cabinet, outlet plate and trim around countertop and backsplash the poppy red of the print. This cheerful new color scheme suggests a batch of bright matching towels, a roundup of amusing thoughts suitable for framing to start the day.

Redeem a bathroom that is definitely dowdy and dated, *below left,* by changing everything but the fixtures. First, enclose the base of the tub and paint molding and tub sides a wild purple. Construct a storage unit to screen the toilet, shelves and towel rails and a high-up medicine cabinet (junk the old one, replace it with a recessed mirror and strips of make-up bulbs). Rip off moldings and sheathe the walls in waterproof vinyl, dropping the high ceiling with vinyl draped over strips of wood, *below right.* Finish it all off by retiring the sloppy shade and café curtains in favor of trim shutters, removing the dangling light and installing a modern ceiling fixture, and giving the floor the sybaritic touch of washable carpet. Courtesy General Tire & Rubber Co.

LOSE AN ATTIC, GAIN A ROOM

Without too expensive or extensive a make-over, an attic or studio at the top of the house can become a snug upstairs pad for a teenager, a guest room or an extra sitting room or TV room.

Keep the furniture low and you don't have to raise the roof to turn your unused attic into a cozy hideaway, *opposite*. By covering the walls with warm, sound-absorbing felt (a real budget material), dark green on side walls, white at ends, you can make the space seem wider, while stick-down parquet tiles can hide the beat-up floor. To give the illusion of a window, hang a double-framed blow-up of a tree on the sloping wall. Pad the floor with a washable nylon rug, use others, cut out, as a wall graphic. Pick lightweight, lightly scaled chairs and tables of plastic and painted wood, a squishy sofa to curl up on, simple lamps. Courtesy Tyndale, Inc.

Add a room by converting the attic to a two-level studio with sleeping and living facilities, *below*. Easy-to-build wood platform and planking floor can be left in the rough with white paint rubbed in to give a pickled finish. Keep up the natural textured look with bamboo blinds, fur rug and throw, wood furniture, plants. Room designed by Fred Palatinus for Bloomingdale's.

Exploit the pitch of an attic room by placing the guest bed dead center, faking a four-poster with 2 x 2's nailed to the exposed beams, *opposite top*. To unify the busy background, use a matching flowered vinyl and fabric throughout the room. Painted floor, "accent rug" and shelves keep floor space uncluttered and easy to clean. Courtesy Wallcovering Industry Bureau.

Put in a plastic bubble to bring height and light to a low-ceilinged attic, *opposite bottom,* and open up the cramped space visually with hound's-tooth patterned fabric and paper in crisp black and white. Table cut down and painted white and other Victorian discards come out of retirement to team with a studio couch, indoor-outdoor carpeting. Room designed by Joan Lerrick. Courtesy American Cyanamid.

Hang the furniture on specially designed pale-oak paneling slotted to support matching chest and shelf units, *below top*. Flank the bed with single panels to hold night tables. To visually double space, mirror the end walls. Designed by Harry Schule and John McCarville. Courtesy Royal System.

Disguise attic beams by extending them to provide twin closets and a niche for the bed; add a shelf as a night table, *below bottom*. Built-ins that conform to awkward architecture are better than storage pieces in space-shy attics. Designed by Lee Bailey for Eastman Chemical.

GIVE A BASEMENT A NEW NAME

Turn the basement into a family room with color, pattern and a fake "window," actually a wall of shutters, shades and tie-back curtains with plants at sill level, *above top*. Add built-in bunks for the kids, adult home comforts of a stove, soft seating, card table and chairs. Courtesy Celanese.
Appoint the basement the teen-age pad where rock can ring out loud and free, *above bottom*. Armor it with plywood paneled walls, indoor-outdoor carpet, floor cushions in place of chairs. Just for kicks, stencil the piano. Designed by Vera Hahn. Courtesy Du Pont.
Tuck a home office down under where there's peace and privacy, soundproof it with an acoustical tile ceiling. You might strip part of the wall of a narrow townhouse basement down to the natural brick as a texture contrast to smooth plywood paneling which boxes in radiator, sewer line and water pipes, *opposite top*. Conceal furnace, storage and mini-seating area behind bifold metal doors, *opposite bottom*. Neat disguise for pipe running along brick wall: clipped-on lights equipped with special bulbs to help the house plants flourish. Courtesy U.S. Plywood.

fruitful labors

There's no doubt about it—the more you can do, the more you can cut costs. These days, thanks to the proliferation of precut, prefinished and prefabricated materials and to the special kits that give your work a professional finish, there's none of that loving-hands-at-home stigma of twenty years ago. Of course, if you are hopeless with a hammer or at sea with a sewing machine, there's not much point in trying to construct a platform or a Parsons table, or sew a slipcover, or do any other job that calls for a certain amount of knowledge or skill; but anyone, all thumbs or no, can sew a heading tape on a prehemmed sheet to make curtains, iron a piece of fabric onto an adhesive-backed shade, or stick mirror tiles on a flat surface. Frequently, that's all you need to do to give your decorating that expensive, custom-made look—which it is, but the service and the secret remain yours.

The rewards of the doer are many, from the virtuous glow of satisfaction at a job well done to the solid capital gains of more money in your pocket. So what better way can you think of to fill a rainy weekend when the beach or the ball game is a wipe-out?

RESHAPE WALLS WITH PAINT...

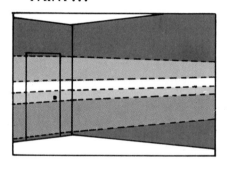

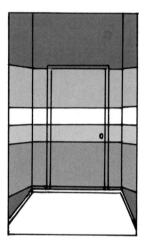

Optical illusion is an important part of decorating and a simple way to correct various problems of interior spaces. The hallway illustrated here was originally an ungainly long and narrow space. Painted in four colors—straight across the door, then tapering down the long walls—the space has been remarkably foreshortened. The painting is easy to do; just outline the stripes in masking tape (one section at a time), paint the section with fast-drying latex paint, and then go on to the next colored stripe. (Courtesy Pittsburgh Paints)

...OR BAMBOO MOLDINGS

A more formal illusion of paneled walls can be created by applying bamboo moldings. You will need 1" half-round split bamboo molding and wire brads. Measure your room and draw lines where you want the panels to go—36" up from the floor for the bottom of a center panel, 28" up from the floor for the top of lower panels. Six inches down from the ceiling is a good height for the top of the center panels as well as for any panels over doors. Wall panels should be approximately 26" to 30" wide, while those over doors are, of course, the width of the door. The panels should start about 6" from the corners of your room and have about 6" between them. Our diagram shows which joints should be mitered and which simply butted.

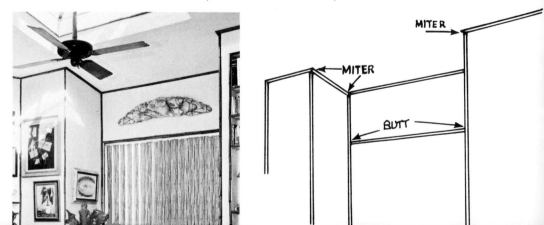

MITER

MITER

BUTT

RENEW OLD FURNITURE WITH PAINT OR FABRIC

The process of reclaiming old furniture—hand-me-downs, Goodwill Industries, Salvation Army, found, unclaimed sales—has always been the most popular of do-it-yourself projects. There is in it the element of discovery, the challenge involved in seeing what can be done with the old wreck, the skills of stripping, sanding, refinishing, painting or reupholstering, and finally the satisfaction of the finished product itself, restored once again to an active part in the decoration of a room.

To do a professional-type paint job, certain rules must be followed. Always work in a well-ventilated, draftless area, whether it be a garage, a basement or a one-room apartment. First cover the floor with a plastic drop-cloth, then spread newspapers on top to catch the gunk. The messiest job is to remove the old coating, paint or finish. If the piece has been previously painted, use nonflammable paint remover, following the directions on the label. Scrubbing with a stiff-bristled brush will get paint off carvings or out of crevices. Clean the surfaces as directed on the paint-remover label. Sand with fine paper, following the grain of the wood. To take off old varnish or shellac, float denatured alcohol over the surface. After a few minutes, rub away the lifted finish with medium-grade steel wool dipped in the alcohol. Then clean off the wood completely with a soft cloth or cheesecloth dipped in alcohol. Let piece dry thoroughly, then sand with fine paper. To prevent old color from showing through if piece has been stained with a particularly penetrating color, give it a white primer coat first to seal it, then the high-gloss enamel.

THREE EASY MAKEOVERS

The cumbersome but useful Victorian chest below was given a new life by stripping off the old finish, then painting it the bright red enamel color of the walls. For a completely different effect, use one of the many antiquing kits and apply the antiquing to highlight the carvings.

The unusual cocktail table below was cut down from a late-Victorian library table and painted a shiny white. Pineapple motif came from upper part of the overly ornate old legs. Alternatively, you might paper the center panel of the top with a *faux*

marbre in one color and the edges in another color, or give it an allover pattern with stencil or peel-and-stick paper.

The no-period bombé chest at the right was transformed by a covering of leopard-print fabric, with top and drawers outlined in black paint. Each leg and post is covered as a unit. Cut four strips of fabric, each one wide enough to wrap around a leg and about 1½" longer than the combined length of the leg and the post to the underside of the top.

Start with the back legs. Lay the chest on its front and apply glue to the bottom surface of one back leg. Placing a strip of material so that the seam will come on the inside edge of the leg, fold 1" of material neatly in under the bottom of the leg and tack it in place. Next apply glue to the leg and post and wrap the fabric completely around the leg (seam to the inner edge), smoothing and pressing out bubbles. On the post, trim off the excess width, leaving only ½" of fabric on either side to press down on the panels and another ½" at the top to press in under the overhang. Do the other back leg, then reverse the chest and repeat for the front legs. Caution: Be sure to remove the bottom tacks before the glue is completely dry.

Next tackle the sides of the chest, cutting the fabric with sharp scissors to fit as neatly as possible. First spread on glue with a brush, then lay on the fabric, pressing out

wrinkles as you do, and tack it in place until it dries. Work on the drawers next (first taking off the pulls), carrying the fabric over the top of each drawer front. Then neatly cut out fabric for the top, allowing enough overlap to go over and under the overhang. Again, brush on glue, lay on fabric, pressing out wrinkles and air bubbles, and tack. When dry, trim around with razor blade. Smooth any exposed edges with fine sandpaper and finally coat the chest with flat varnish or clear plastic. For use in another room, you could stencil an overscaled wood-grain design on top, sides and drawers, painting posts and legs and outlining drawers in contrasting color.

TRANSFORM YOUR ROOMS THROUGH STENCILING...

Stenciling—a recent revival of an old art—is an attractive and creative way to give zing to rooms and furniture that have begun to bore you. Mushy architectural detail can be sharpened or obscured (your decision) by a brisk repetition of geometric patterns —on floors, walls, windows, or furniture.

...A WINDOW SHADE

To get in practice you might start with window-shade stenciling. You'll need stencil paper, stencil knife, stencil brushes, Prang Textile Colors, masking tape, an old plate for color mixing, and cleanup materials—Textile Cleaner and Extendor and rags. One of the best approaches to stencil design is to pattern it after an existing motif in your room. The most important thing to remember about the design you choose—when you're doing the actual work you'll be thankful you did—is *keep it simple*.

To start, trace or draw your design on stencil paper with a 2" margin all around it. Make a separate stencil for each color, and cut out the designs with the sharp stencil knife.

Place the stencils, one at a time, in position on the shade and tape them in place with masking tape.

Mix the color you desire and add an equal amount of Extendor to the paint. Then dip the stencil brush in the color and wipe off most of the paint on a spare piece of paper (the brush must not be too wet when applied to the stencil). Holding the brush in a vertical position and working

color onto the surface with a circular motion, start at the edge of the stencil opening and work toward the center (so that the color will not bleed under the edge of the stencil). Then carefully lift the stencil off and wait for the first color to dry before applying the second stencil and color over it. Be sure to clean your brush thoroughly in the Tex-

tile Cleaner before re-using it for another color.

Allow your finished prints to dry for 24 hours, then set them with a warm iron for permanency. With your iron set at a low temperature, and a dry pressing cloth between the iron and the shade, go over each section of the design for six minutes. (Courtesy Window Shade Mfrs. Assn.)

...A WOOD FLOOR

If you're feeling the urge to stencil a bigger surface, such as a floor, here is a versatile stencil design, originated for *House Beautiful*, that can be adapted to a variety of looks and may give you some ideas for your own original stencils. One 9"-square stencil, angled in four different directions, is all it takes to do the allover trellis design of triangles inside squares shown on page 169. The directions we give apply to any wood floor.

First sand the floor to remove wax, varnish, or the old finish. To keep the floor free of dust and marks during the entire stenciling process, wear socks, not shoes, when you work.

Prepare the background in one of three ways—leave the natural wood, cover it with flat or semi-gloss paint (acrylic, oil-based, or latex), or stain it.

Divide the floor into 9" squares (we choose this repeat because many floors are made up of 9"

parquet tiles and, thus, are pre-measured for you). If your room divides more easily into 8", 10" or 12" squares, by all means just change the size of the stencil accordingly.

Next take a 15" square of waxed stencil paper and draw a 9" square in the middle of it (get larger stencil paper if you increase the size of your design, so there will always be a margin around it). In each corner of the 9" square draw a right triangle ½" from the edge

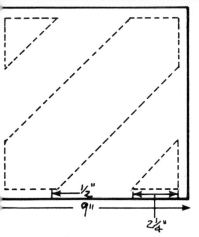

and 2¼" long on each leg. The hexagon in the middle is made by simply connecting the base angles of the two triangles that are catty-cornered to each other. Next place the stencil paper on a glass surface and, with a razor blade or a stencil knife, cut out the three shapes. Tape the stencil to the precise middle of your floor so that the design will radiate evenly toward the walls (irregularities on the edges of the room are common-place, but one in the middle is an eyesore). Roll a mohair paint roller with very little paint on it across the stencil pattern. Use either flat or semigloss latex or oil-base paint, thinned respectively with water or turpentine, so it will dry quickly.

Lift the stencil and tape it carefully to the next square you want to paint. (Always skip a square so as not to risk smearing the square you just completed.) Repeat the stenciling until you cover as much area as you desire. The paint will dry very quickly, but allow it to "mellow" or "cure" for about three days. At the end of that time seal in the design with at least two coats of a satin-finish polyurethane varnish.

Floor stencils—both this and your own designs—can be used in many ways for many different looks. For an area-rug effect, you can paint a striped, scalloped, or fringed border. To enlarge the dimensions of a favorite rug, you might edge its perimeter with stenciled rows, perhaps repeating the pattern or color on the furniture grouped around it. Or in *trompe l'oeil* fashion, you could stencil a design in a hall or down a flight of stairs to look like a runner. (Courtesy *House Beautiful*)

WHERE TO BUY STENCIL KITS

If you are nervous about measuring and cutting your own patterns, you can buy precut stencils in most art-supply stores. Complete kits are available from American Decorative Arts, Inc., Box 284, Cold Spring Harbor, N.Y. 11724; two others come from stencil artists Cile Lord and Adele Bishop, who did the stenciled floor on page 18. One is called The Bishop & Lord Stencil Deluxe Home Decorating Kit, the other, Stencil Art Kit; both are available at Bloomingdale's, or write to Rochman Imports, Inc., 102 West 75 Street, Room 70, New York, N.Y. 10023. These ladies also have three other Home Decorator Kits— for walls, furniture, boxes and tinware. Bill Bell, one of whose designs is shown on page 27, has come up with a kit based on a more advanced form of stenciling, where paint is poured into the top of a frame containing a silkscreen design set on aluminum tracks. A piece of rubber-tipped molding called a squeegee is pulled across the screen, pressing the pigment through the silk to leave a pattern on the surface below. The kit allows you more intricate patterns and greater precision in application as well as speeding up the whole process. After stripping a small floor of wax and varnish, it takes about four hours for a one-color pattern, six for two colors, then eighteen for the paint to cure before adding your final coating of polyurethane varnish. You can get Bill Bell's Screen Printing Kit at Bloomingdale's, or write to Bill Bell Designs, Inc., 27 East 50 Street, New York, N.Y. 10022

HOW TO FAKE A FOUR-POSTER

New sheets in fanciful patterns can be the springboard for many easy, decorative ideas, especially in bedrooms and bathrooms. For instance, if you yearn for a four-poster but can't afford one, consider making a framework above the bed from which you can hang sheets at the four corners. When you're finished, you'll have the whole effect without the posts.

You will need: 1" X 2" pine strips equal to the dimensions of your bed (single, double or other), six to ten queen-size sheets, an equal yardage of lining material, small-headed tacks, toggle bolts, approximately 48 hooks and screw eyes, 2" pleater tape.

1 Securing it with the toggle bolts, attach a rectangle of the 1" X 2" strips to the ceiling above your bed. The frame should be an inch wider and an inch longer than the bed itself. Cover the framework by stretching a sheet across it and tacking the material around the edges.

2 On the undersurface, around each corner of the frame, insert 12 screw eyes (a larger size of the variety you find on picture frames) approximately 2" apart. The number of screw eyes and the distance between them will depend on how wide you want your "posts." This will also determine whether you use one or two sheets per corner.

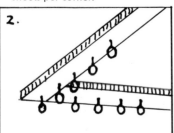

The lining should be cut to the same length as the sheeting, but 2" narrower. Seam the sheets and lining material together along their sides with the right sides together and wide hems on the bottom.

Turn right side out and press.

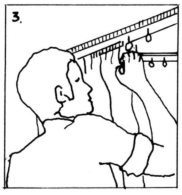

Following the manufacturer's instructions, apply pleater tape along the top edge of each set of sheets, insert the hooks and hook the "posts" to the screw eyes on the frame—**3.**

Once the curtains are up, measure all around the perimeter of the frame to determine the length needed for a valance. The depth of the valance is a matter of personal taste, but should not be less than 8". Place sheet and lining right sides together and seam three sides, leaving one short end open. Turn right side out and press. Turn in the open end and close it with a row of top stitching. With small-headed tacks, attach the valance around the frame to cover the hooks. (4) You can either work the fibers of the material over the tack heads to conceal them, or cover the tacks with a length of braid trimming. (Courtesy Stevens-Utica)

HOW TO CONSTRUCT A PLATFORM

To make the mirror-covered platforms that hold the étagères shown on page 48 you will need, for the larger unit: two ½" plywood lengths 6' X 8", seven ½" plywood lengths 1'11" X 8", and one large ½" plywood panel 6' X 2'. With the two 6' lengths and two of the 1'11" lengths, construct a rectangular box base by nailing the corners at approximately 2" intervals. Then, at 1' intervals along the box, nail the remaining five 1'11" lengths across the rectangle for support. Finally, the large 6' X 2' panel of plywood is nailed to the top of the box.

For the smaller unit you need two ½" plywood lengths 3' X 8", four ½" plywood lengths 2'11" X 8", and a top panel of ½" plywood 3' square. Construct a square with the two longer lengths and two of the shorter ones, nailing them together at the corners. Place the two remaining short lengths at 1' intervals within the square and nail them together for support. Then nail the top piece on.

Place the two components of the platform side by side on the floor with the 3'-square unit in the

corner of the room. Three-inch-square mirror tiles (from Sears) can then be affixed to the bases with the tape squares that come with the tiles. To fit the tiles on the 8" base you will need a simple glass cutter (or if you wish, you may make the base 12" to avoid cutting).

The tiles on the wall of the room are also affixed with tape. The wall with mirror strips has one 9" wide, one 6" wide, and one 3" wide, outlined by a firring strip painted white. (Courtesy Sears)

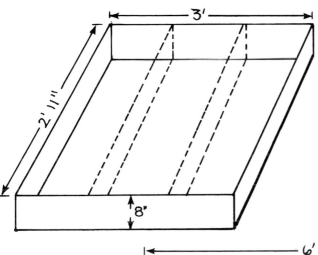

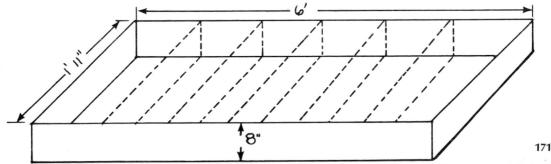

ALL ABOUT WALL COVERINGS

Recent developments in wall-covering materials have exploded old arguments that wallpaper is too fragile, too hard to hang, too expensive, can't be cleaned, fades too fast, and is hard to remove. Since walls are the largest area of a room and can make a tremendous impact on its overall look, when you want to do your own decorating it's a good idea to consider some of the new wall coverings.

Prepasted papers have existed for at least twenty-five years, but the new ones are something special. The designs are well drawn and sophisticated in all price ranges. Costs compare favorably with moderately priced unpasted papers, and the expense of adhesives or paperhangers is eliminated. Do-it-yourself techniques are clearly explained in brochures available when you purchase your paper—and many prepasted coverings are also strippable.

Strippable coverings, stronger than the adhesives that hold them to the wall, are a blend of cellulose, latex, resins, synthetic and natural fibers with, often, a resilient vinyl face coating and/or a fiber backing. They're easy to install and peel off quickly for changes—making them a good investment.

Vinyl coverings are made from a liquid that is either pressed into a film or coated onto a backing of paper or fabric. The advantages are durability, cleanability, and the ease with which it can be removed to make way for new decoration.

Peel-and-stick plastics have the advantage of needing no water, paste, buckets, brushes, or seam rollers—and they can be applied on many surfaces where paper can't. As they are sold by the yard, there is little waste.

To produce a result you are proud of when covering your walls, it is important to remember that the surface must be grease-free and that any and all old wall coverings must be removed—along with all traces of old paste. To prepare a previously painted wall, chip off the old paint and spackle any holes, then seal with glue sizing. Unpainted plaster and paper-surfaced wallboard should also be sized before papering. An oil-base-painted surface should be sanded first, while new plywood must be shellacked or oil-base-painted before applying a wall covering. Be sure to paint all the trim in your room before hanging the wallpaper. Then follow to the letter the manufacturer's directions for hanging.

HOW TO MEASURE FOR WALLPAPER AND BORDER PAPERS

Size of Room* in feet	7 ft.	Wall Height to Ceiling 8 or 9 ft.	10, 11 or 12 ft.	Ceiling	Border 4 sides
		Number of Single Rolls Needed			Yards
6 x 10	7	8	11	3	12
6 x 12, or 8 x 10	8	9	12	3	13
8 x 12	8	10	14	3	13
8 x 14, or 10 x 12	9	11	15	4	15
9 x 12	9	11	15	5	16
9 x 14	10	12	16	5	17
9 x 16	11	13	18	5	18
10 x 14, or 12 x 12	10	12	16	5	17
10 x 16, or 12 x 14	11	13	18	6	19
12 x 16, or 12 x 14	12	14	19	7	20
12 x 18, or 14 x 16	12	15	20	7	21
14 x 18, or 16 x 16	13	16	22	8	23
16 x 18	14	17	23	8	24
16 x 20	15	18	24	10	25
	For walls			For ceiling	

*Deduct one single roll for every two doors or windows of average size in the room—or deduct two single rolls for every three openings counted.

IT'S EASY TO...
...MAKE YOUR OWN FABRIC SHADE

If you've admired the custom look of shades matched to upholstery or a bedspread, take heart—there's no trick to it. All you need is adhesive-backed Tontine shade cloth, to which you laminate your own fabric by pressing the two together with an iron.

Decide how you want to mount the shade on the window frame and measure the distance between the metal brackets (this is called the barrel measure). The roller should be at least 1⅛" in diameter. The 1¼" wood slat for the bottom of the shade matches the length of the roller inside its metal rings (this is the cloth measure). You will need: Tontine shade cloth, fabric, non-waxy tailor's chalk, a steel tape measure, a yardstick, a sharp pencil, long-blade shears, masking tape and a steam iron. It's best to do the work on a large table covered with sheeting.

Cut the fabric 6" longer than the height of the window opening (to allow a pocket for the wooden slat), and 1″ wider than the finished shade (for evening and trimming). Straighten the top by following the design with a yardstick. Press the fabric carefully; remove all ravelings and lint. If using a steam iron, remove all water! Moisture may shrink or stretch the fabric. Mark the center of the fabric, top and bottom, with the chalk. The Tontine shade cloth should be cut 18″ longer than the window height and 2″ wider than the finished shade. From the length of this piece cut off a 2″ and an 8″ strip for slat and roller attachments.

A Place the Tontine cloth on the work table with adhesive side up. Remove the liner paper and save for pressing, marking the center, top and bottom. Measure down 2″ from the top and draw a line across.

B Place the top edge of the fabric on the marked line and smooth it over the Tontine, aligning center marks at top and bottom. Secure the corners. Set iron to proper fabric temperature and test it on scraps. If the fabric setting is too cool for proper bonding, turn the

shade over and—using the liner paper—press the Tontine side as well. Work from the center to the edges in short strokes, pressing hard. Never touch the iron to the Tontine! Check to be sure no areas have been missed; then cool the shade to room temperature.

C Proper alignment and trimming is a critical step. A shade which is not accurately measured and trimmed to size may roll off center—or not at all. For thick fabrics, the shade should be ½″ less than the barrel measure of the roller, for sheers ¼″ less. With chalk, mark the finished width on the fabric edge of the shade. Use your yardstick to draw a line down each side of the shade to outline the width. Check again before cutting with smooth, even strokes. Square off if necessary.

To prepare slat hem, draw a line 1¼″ from the bottom edge with the chalk and turn the hem to the Tontine side. Fold along the line and anchor the ends with masking tape. Using the liner paper, press the hem edge, being sure not to press the Tontine directly with the iron. Place the 2″ strip of Tontine

along the folded edge of the hem line, using the chalk line as a guide. One inch should extend beyond each side edge and a small margin will extend beyond the hem edge.

D Put liner paper down and press lightly. Insert the wood slat and press firmly with the iron along the upper edge of the slat. Let the shade cool and trim it.

Remove the liner from the 8″ strip of Tontine. Adhesive side down, place the lower edge of the strip so it meets the top edge of the fabric and secure the corners. Press with iron through liner paper the 2″ where the bare Tontine meets the strip. Allow to cool. Remeasure edge of Tontine to be sure it is parallel with the upper edge of the fabric.

E Place the upper edge of the Tontine strip along the black line of the roller. Cover with liner and press lightly. Wind the Tontine over the roller surface, constantly pressing to get a complete bond, until you reach the end of the adhesive. Your shade is ready to install. (Courtesy Window Shade Mfrs. Assn.)

A B C

D E

IT'S EASY TO
...CREATE A VERTICAL BLIND

Thanks to a new design from Thru-Vu Vertical Blind Corp., it is now easy to install your own vertical blinds. The kit, called the NH (for no hem) Simplicity Model, is custom assembled to fit any kind of window, and is particularly effective with sliding window-door panels and picture windows. Plastic-coated fabric louvers come in a long roll in a wide variety of fabrics and colors, and can be cut to fit any window length. After you have cut a strip the proper length for your window (1), you simply slip the ends of the louvers into special plastic holders (2) that screw into bar latches on the horizontal tracks (3). The kit is available from Thru-Vu Vertical Blind Corp., Mamaroneck, New York 10543.

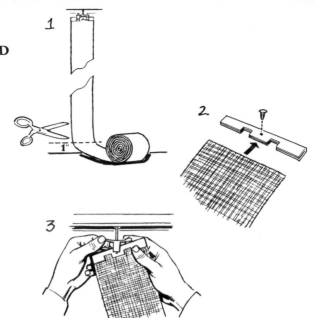

...TRIM A PLAIN SHADE

Appliqués and trims on window shades are an excellent way to tie various motifs in your room together. Closely woven fabrics—polished cotton, chintz and percale—are best for appliques. When doing smaller cutouts, keep raw edges from raveling by first painting the cutting line on the back with colorless nail polish. If you want to do large designs, spray the back of the fabric with a clear acrylic spray, such as Krylon, or press iron-on Pelonite onto the back of the appliqué. Be sure to test your fabric first, because some fibers—notably acetate—will dissolve.

Cut out your designs carefully and arrange them as a completed pattern on the shade. Then, one at a time, apply glue to the reverse side and press the cutout onto the shade. Smooth it carefully, checking for loose edges and air bubbles. After the design is complete and dry, an additional coat of clear acrylic spray can be an added protection.

Trims for shades offer staggering variety—fringes, braids, gimp, tape, ribbons, eyelet edging, rickrack, printed borders from fabrics, decorative shade pulls, shade-cloth valances. To avoid wrinkling

trim you choose, do not try to sew the trimming on, either by hand or by machine. Adhesive is much safer and equally effective, and the one recommended for fixing both your shades when you apply the

appliqués and trims is Bond Cement #693. It can be ordered from J. Padovani, 94-10 64th Road, Rego Park, N.J. 11374, at $1.00 for a 3¼-ounce tube. (Courtesy Window Shade Mfrs. Assn.)

...TAKE THE MEASURE OF SHADES

Measuring correctly for window shades, venetian blinds and woven shades is both important and exacting. First of all, you should use a wooden or metal ruler; cloth tape is too flexible.

To measure the width for a new window shade to hang inside the window casement, measure the exact distance between the points where the brackets are to be placed (A). On your order, specify IB (inside bracket) mounting—the factory will allow for bracket clearance.

If you want the shade to hang outside the window casement, measure between the points where the brackets are to be placed—they should be positioned to allow 1½" to 2" overlap on each side of the casement (B). Again, be sure to specify OB (outside bracket) mounting on your order.

To measure the length of your window, measure from the top of the frame (soffit) to top of the sill and add 12" (D). The extra 12" is the safety margin that allows the shade to be pulled to full length without being torn from the roller.

If shade is to be hung from ceiling, measure from ceiling down to top of sill (E) for length. For width, measure to outer edges of casing (C).

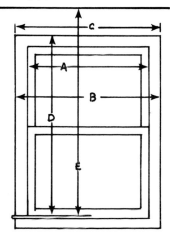

When replacing old shades, measure from tip to tip, including the little metal pins on each end. Specify "tip to tip" on your order.

Decorative trims such as scallops or fringe at the bottom should be added to the length

dimension given so that they will rest against the sill and ensure privacy. (Instructions and sketch: Window Shade Mfrs. Assn.)

...AND BLINDS

To measure the width of venetian blinds to hang inside the window casing, measure exact distance between inside edges of window casing (A). Do not make allowances as slats and bottom rail will be made slightly narrower at the factory to prevent rubbing against casing. Headbox will also be made narrower to fit installation brackets. Be sure to specify IB (inside blinds) on your order.

To measure the length of your window, measure distance from the top of the frame (soffit) to top of the lower sill (B). As the manufacturer makes no deduction in length, you may wish to make blind-length dimension ½" shorter to avoid touching sill. If there is no sill, or blind is to overlap the sill, measure (E) to point to which blind is to reach.

If you want the blinds to hang on the outside of the window casing or the wall, measure the exact distance (C) between points where brackets are to be placed. Brackets need 1"-wide flat surface for mounting. Measurement (C) should be at least 3" more than measurement (A) for privacy. Be sure to specify OB on order for this type of blind.

To find the length, measure exact distance (D) between point where top of brackets will be and top of sill. If there is no sill, or the blind is to overlap the sill, measure (F) down to point blind is to reach.

To measure a door for blinds, follow directions as for OB (outside bracket) but specify "for door" on order, since these require hold-down brackets to keep the blind from swaying when the door is opened or closed. These brackets may also be ordered as an "extra" for window blinds to prevent swaying in the breeze. Be sure to specify on your order whether brackets at each end of the bottom rail are to be fastened to top of sill, inside the jambs, or to the face of the casing, door or wall.

To measure width of woven

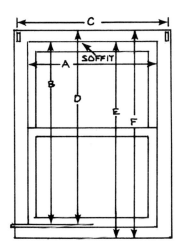

aluminum shades to hang inside the window casing, measure exact distance between inside edges (A). Do not make any allowance, as shades will be made slightly narrower to prevent rubbing against casing.

To measure the length, take exact distance between top of frame (soffit) and top of sill (B). If there is no sill, or shade is to overlap the sill, measure to point to which shade is to reach (E). Specify IB installation on your order.

To find width of blind to be installed on the outside face of window casing or wall, measure exact distance between points where brackets are to be placed (C). Again, this should be at least 3" more than measurement (A) for privacy.

To measure length, take exact distance between point where top of shade, including roller, will be placed and top of sill (D). If there is no sill, or shade is to overlap the sill, take measurement (F) down to point shade is to reach. The factory will include extra "wrap-around" for roller. (Instructions and sketch: Levelor-Lorentzen)

TWO SMART IDEAS FOR FURNITURE:

THE STRIPCOVER...

Here's a close-up of how the smooth, close-fitting double-knit polyester slipcovers shown on page 68 zip off for cleaning.

1. Unzip the covers and slip out the cushions.
2. Lift out the upholstered seating platform.
3. Detach the Velcro tabs along the frame.
4. Pull open the Velcro-attached side seam.
5. Now remove the cover in one easy motion.
6. Sofa and seat covers ready for washing or cleaning.

(Courtesy Kroehler)

1

2

3

4

5

6

...AND THE EASY-FIT, DOUBLE-KNIT SLIPCOVER

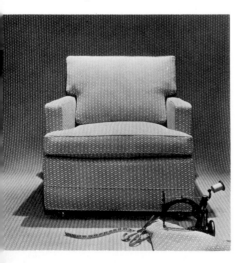

New polyester double-knit fabrics have given the art of slipcovering a great boost. The stretch factor in these fabrics both simplifies fitting and stitching and makes the covers hug the contours of the furniture to give it an upholstered look never before possible. Polyester double knits may at first seem expensive, but they are generous in width (usually 60" or 63") and welting, if used, is cut on the crosswise grain, saving on fabric, time, and cost. In addition, most of these knits are machine-washable, no-iron, shape-retentive, and abrasion-resistant.

DETERMINING YARDAGE

First decide what knit fabric you want to buy, discover its width, measure the pieces you will need for your chair (or whatever) and make a simple yardage graph and pattern diagram to find out how much fabric you'll need.

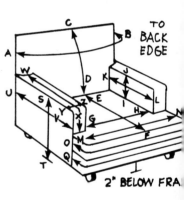

MEASURING

To measure for a chair cover, use the seams of the original chair covering as a guide. To allow for the stretch factor, subtract ¾" from both length and width of all pieces except arm strips and cushion strips. Add 1" seam allowance on each piece— ½" seams are ample. For tuck-in add 3" at points D, E, G, H, I and K.

The seat-cushion front strip should be measured from the line at M-O around the front to the same point on the other side.

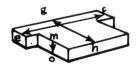

Sides of the cushion will be seamed here. Measure back strip from this point—two strips one-half the width will be needed with 1″ additional on each piece as a seam allowance for the zipper or Velcro closing. Measure the length of all seams where the welting will be used.

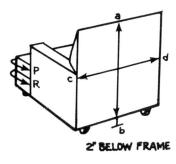

2″ BELOW FRAME

FITTING

Centering the pieces and keeping the grain of the fabric straight, pin outside and inside backs to chair (right side out because you cannot depend on symmetry). Pin from center to outside edges, gently and evenly stretching the fabric

MITER CORNERS

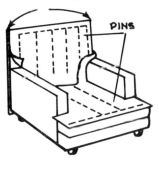

PINS

to fit (this should be done *only* with double-knit polyesters). Pin seams at points A, B, and C, mitering corners. At bottom of inside back allow for a 3″ tuck-in, trimming edge upward until fabric narrows to only ½″ seam allowance at top of arms. Pin seat section and fold tuck-in back, trimming to 3″. Cut fabric to T-shape with ½″ seam allowance at front of arms. Pin tuck-ins of back and seat together at edges for seaming.

Next pin outside arm, arm strip and inside arm sections to chair, with seam allowances where these sections join each other. Pin arm to seat section, leaving 3″ allowance along the sides and ½″ at front of arms. Where arm joins inside back, pin snugly at arm top, then along tuck-in allowance to the bottom. Pin front strips to seat and outside arms. Pin back of outside arms to outside back.

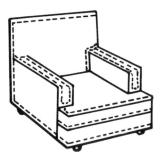

Tuck in allowance all around seat and check chair for fit, adjusting where necessary. Spread all the seams and tuck-ins open, and, using chalk or pins, mark seam allowance on the wrong sides. Before unpinning from the chair, cut notches in seam allowances at center edge of each piece to facilitate matching pieces for seaming. Unpin seams. Stitch welting in place. Then pin slipcover sections together, right sides facing, and stitch in the same order in which the pieces were fitted.

On the cushion, sew the strips for the zipper opening first. At both ends of strips, pin 1″ seam allowance, leaving a long enough opening in the center section for

ZIPPER

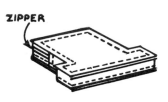

the zipper. Machine-baste the opening and sew in the zipper. Join one end of the zipper strip to the front strip. Topstitch the seam. Sew welting to both edges of joined strips.

Pin the cushion top and bottom in place. Pin to strip all around. Pin remaining ends of strips, cutting seam allowance to ½″ if necessary. Spread seams and mark allowances with chalk or pins on the wrong side. Stitch seams along the stitching line that holds the welting in place. Topstitch seam in the strip. Repeat for the back cushion if there is one.

CUTTING, MARKING, SEWING, AND FINISHING

The strength and durability of polyester fibers makes them hard to cut. Use a very sharp scissors and wipe the blades often to free them of lint. Label each piece for easy identification when sewing. Whether sewing on a straight-stitch or a zigzag machine, you will need a looser tension than usual and possibly less pressure on the presser foot for a smooth seam. If welting is used, stitch it to the smaller sections first, then to the construction seams—don't try to do all in one operation. Our chair is finished at the bottom by turning the 2″ allowance to the underside of the chair. Pin-miter the four corners. Then cut away the fabric that forms the miter. Stitch a strip of Velcro to the underfold and tack a matching strip of Velcro to the wooden frame.

(Instruction sketches and photographs courtesy *Family Circle*.)

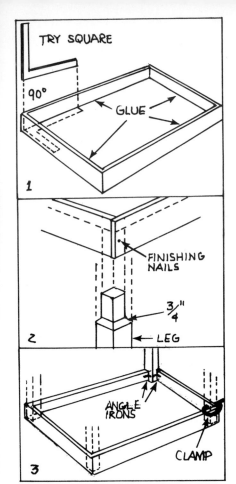

TRY SQUARE

90°

GLUE

1

FINISHING NAILS

$\frac{3}{4}''$

LEG

2

ANGLE IRONS

CLAMP

3

HOW TO CONSTRUCT A PARSONS TABLE...

The Parsons table, designed in the 20's at the Parsons School of Design in New York (and alternatively called the T-square table), is for many reasons the Ford of the contemporary decorating world. Its simple unadorned lines fit in with almost any kind of furniture or style of decoration. If kept in the proper proportion, it can be made to serve almost any purpose that you can come up with and look good in the process. It is important to note that the proper Parsons table looks like one solid piece of wood—since the apron and legs are the same width.

Our instructions are for a rectangular table 24" wide, 44" long, and 29" high. You will need one ¾" X 22½" X 42½" plywood top; two ¾" X 3" X 44" lengths of clear pine (for the length of the apron); two ¾" X 3" X 22½" lengths of clear pine (width of the apron); four 3" X 3" x 28¼" lengths of Italian poplar or clear pine (for the legs); three dozen 2" finishing nails; a try square; four 3" angle irons; wood filler; glue; and some fine, medium, and coarse sandpaper.

1. Lay the table top on your floor or worktable and stand the apron pieces around it. Attach the apron to the table top with wood glue, checking with the try square to make sure that each corner is an exact 90° angle.

2. Taking an end of each table leg, measure down 2½" and cut two adjoining grooves at a 90° angle ¾" deep. Fit the grooved end into a corner of the top and sides to be sure the leg fits tightly. Apply wood glue to the grooves and along the edge of the apron. Attach the legs and check with the try square to see that the alignment is correct. Hold the corner tight for a few minutes until the glue is set—or keep clamps fastened on the legs for a few hours. To reinforce the table, mark finishing-nail holes ⅜" from the edge of each apron piece and ⅜" from the top and bottom edges. Countersink all nails.

3. For stability, screw angle irons into each corner. Fill all holes, and sand table perfectly smooth before painting with lacquer.

...AND COVER IT WITH FABRIC

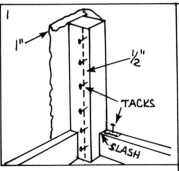

1

1"

½"

TACKS

SLASH

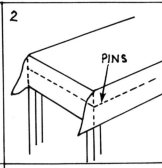

2

PINS

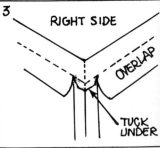

3

RIGHT SIDE

OVERLAP

TUCK UNDER

If you'd rather not paint, with its attendant sanding and priming, cover the table with fabric. For this you'll need a 36" fabric, scissors, glue and tacks. Again our instructions are for a 24" X 44" table.

1. Do the legs first. Cut enough fabric to cover the length of the leg up to the top of the table plus 1" (29¼" in all) and the girth of the leg plus 1" (or 13"). Fold and press the fabric 1" under for the bottom of the leg. Fold and press fabric ½" under along one length of the leg. Wrap it around the leg, placing the unfolded edge ½" over the inside edge of the leg. Glue and tack. As you wrap, clip fabric as it meets the edge of the apron. Glue and tack. Be sure to remove all your tacks before the glue is completely dry.

2. For the table top, place the fabric wrong side up on the table and cut it to cover the top and overlap to the inside of the apron. Pin darts at each corner of the top piece so it covers the table like a slipcover. Stitch the darts, cut away the excess material in the darts,

reverse the cover, and place it on the table.

3. Clip the top piece at points where the apron meets the legs and tuck the fabric under where it covers the legs at the corners. Fold the overlap edges of the top piece around and up inside the apron. Glue and tack—again removing the tacks before the glue dries.

It is a good idea to have a glass top made for your table to protect the fabric from spotting and staining.

(Instructions and sketches courtesy Conso Publishing Co.)

HOW TO CONSTRUCT A CUBE

To make cubes like those shown on page 17, for each one take a 4' X 8' X ½" sheet of plywood and cut five pieces from it as follows:

For the top, one piece 24" X 24". Two side pieces 24" X 23½" and two more side pieces 23½" X 23". Fit the pieces together to form a perfect 24" square. Glue and then nail the pieces together with small finishing nails. Sand the edges smooth, removing any loose splinters. Fill any cracks or holes with a patching paste. When dry, sand lightly. Apply a primer coat to all surfaces.

Now you can paint your cubes, marbleize them with an antiquing kit, cover them with découpage, self-adhesive paper or vinyl, glue on sheets of 1" mirror squares (those on page 17 were covered with Mylar), or give them a wood-tone finish, using a kit.

HOW TO FRAME A WINDOW WITH A LATTICE...

An interesting effect can be created by building a lattice frame around a large window. You will need 1" X 1" lengths of clear pine cut to the dimensions your window requires, 1¼" finishing nails, and four 1½" flat-head wood screws.

First cut the pine lengths required to fit around the window opening and screw them together at the corners. Then cut the lengths of the *outer* frame of the trellis and screw them together. The criss-cross pieces of the trellis are determined in size, of course, by the size of the frame. They have both ends cut at 45° angles. You simply criss-cross the pieces and nail them to the outer frame to create the design shown in the diagram. Then paint your trellis and nail it to the frame or wall around the window.

...OR A FABRIC

You can also enliven a window by framing it in fabric. For one window, you will need: one piece of 1" X 10" pine the width of the window, two pieces of 1" X 10" pine the height of the window, 1"-thick Dacron-filled padding, tacks or staples, mending plates, toggle bolts (if needed), plus your fabric.

Before cutting the fabric be sure to check that the boards are the proper size. For the top piece, cut 15" strips across the full width of the fabric. Joining the strips on the 15" edges so that the design matches, seam them together until the piece is long enough to go across the full width of the top piece. Press seams flat. (Diagram 1.) Cover the front face only with padding, stapling it to the board. Then cover with fabric, mitering the corners, and tack or staple to the back. (Diagram 2.)

For the side pieces, cut 15" strips of fabric to the length required and cover in same manner as for top piece, matching the design where it meets the top piece. Attach top to side pieces with mending plates, then nail side pieces to wall if there are studs, or use toggle bolts. (Diagram 3.) (Courtesy McCall's; Photograph by Grigsby)

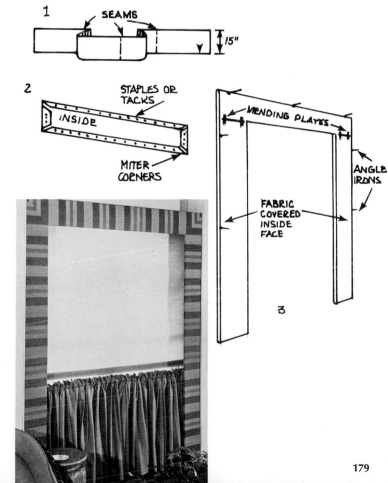

the 1¼" hem with 2" heavy-duty double-stick masking tape (working on a flat surface). As soon as one side is finished apply to the wall. The thickness of the fabric and the heavy tape will hold firm and give a sharp finished edge. (Dusting with a clean brush or whisk broom will make only occasional laundering necessary. When you do remove the coverings for laundering, simply remove the tape and replace it with new tape.)

For the shower curtain, use one queen-size sheet cut off at 6" and hemmed on all four sides. A grommet kit from the hardware store punches in metal grommets for the curtain rings, and the curtain is hung over a plastic liner.

For the underskirt and overskirt for the sink, use the leftover fabric from the shower curtain and a contrasting single sheet. First measure the perimeter of the basin counter top. Cut the leftover fabric to fit this measurement plus allowances for hemming the sides and bottom. Measure the contrasting sheet the same way, adding half again as much to the length. Hem the short piece. Split the contrasting top skirt into four even panels after sewing hem edges, then sew the two fabrics together, using a ruffling attachment to make the top ruffled edge. Attach the completed skirt with Velcro, gluing the rigid portion to the stand and sewing the flexible portion to the inside top of the skirt. Tie back the contrasting overskirt with braid.

For the window shade use a single sheet in the original pattern and a Lam-Eze window-shade kit, which comes in widths up to 46" at hardware and shade stores. Line up the shade cloth and the fabric, peel back the plastic covering on the Lam-Eze and unroll the fabric onto the adhesive surface. Smooth the fabric with the palms of your hands and cut away the excess.

The bathroom carpet we used also came in a 6' X 9' kit. Scraps of leftover material of any kind can be used to cover tissue boxes, waste baskets, and other bathroom accessories. (Instructions and photograph: Celanese)

THE WELL-DRESSED BATHROOM WEARS SHEETS...

In the last few years sheets as an element of decoration have really come into their own, erupting in a startling variety of patterns. With all this design change, an enormous price increase might have been expected, but sheets are still a bargain—and, for uses other than on beds, much cheaper than equal amounts of most upholstery fabrics. Another plus is their width. How often can you find a length of fabric 108" X 115"? The chart on the opposite page shows the many sizes sheets come in today.

Your imagination will probably suggest many fabric uses for sheet-ing, and we show here only a few ideas to get you started. To decorate the 6' X 6' bathroom on page 102 we used: four queen-size sheets, two single sheets, a Lam-Eze shade kit, a grommet kit, 5 yards of trimming, and 1½ yards of Velcro. The walls and ceiling were covered with three queen-size sheets (with contrasting colored or patterned hems removed). Here's how to do it.

Measure wall and ceiling dimensions carefully and cut pieces for each, allowing an extra 1¼" to fold under. Match the pattern repeat carefully before you cut. Sew pieces together. Turn under

...WHICH ALSO SKIRT A ROUND TABLE

Drip-dry sheets are particularly good for covering tables to the floor. They are easy to work with, keep their crispness and shape, and wash like a dream. Added bonus: bright, interesting colors and patterns. Finish the hem, if you like, with solid-color fringe.

First remove 1" hem at the bottom of the sheet by cutting along the stitching. Fold the sheet in half lengthwise, then fold crosswise to form a rectangle four layers thick. To obtain the radius of the cover, add twice the table height to the table diameter; then divide in half. Make a string compass—tie a knot at one end of a string and a second knot at a point from the first equal to the radius. Pin one knot of the compass at the center corner of the folded edges and mark a semicircle at the length of the second knot for the cut line. Cut along the line through *all* the thicknesses.

To make facings for the bottom of the skirt, remove the hem along the top edge of the sheet and press sheet to remove the fold lines. Using the circle as a pattern, mark half-circle for facing A (see diagram) and quarter-

circles for facings B and C. Make them 3" wide and allow ½" at each end for seams. With right sides together and making ½" seams, join the facings to make a circle. Press the seams flat. Stitch around the inside edges of the facing with a small stitch, then pink the edge. With the right sides together, place the facing around the sheet circle and stitch around the outside edge ½" in from the edge. Turn right side out and press with the seam on the exact edge of the sheet. Then hem the top edge of the facing of the sheet.

Incidentally, if you are using a king-size sheet the lower edge need not be faced, since there is

enough material to form a deep hem. You must first remove the stiching from the top hem and press to remove the fold. Then fold the sheet to form a rectangle four layers thick. Draw a circle as for the other sheet; then mark a second line 2½" outside the first line for the cut line. Turn ½" to wrong side and hem, easing in fullness. This method may be used for other sheets too, if they are wide enough (depending on table size).

The chart tells you what size sheets to buy for tables 24" or 30" high of different diameters, and also how much fringe will be needed. (Instructions and sketches: Springs Mills)

SHEET SIZES FOR ROUND TABLECLOTHS	
Tables 24" high	
up to 24" diameter	one twin plus 6½ yds. fringe
up to 33" diameter	one double plus 7½ yds.
up to 42" diameter	one queen plus 8 yds.
up to 54" diameter	one king plus 9 yds.
Tables 30" high	
up to 21" diameter	one double plus 7 yds.
up to 30" diameter	one queen plus 8 yds.
up to 42" diameter	one king plus 9 yds.

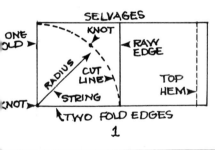

1

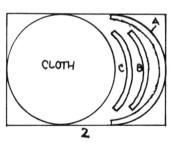

2

SIZE GUIDE FOR SHEETS

Mattress	Flat	Fitted	Blanket
0 x 75 (cot)	66 x 104	30 x 75	50 x 60 robe
3 x 75 (day bed)	66 x 104	33 x 75	66 x 90
6 x 75 (single)	66 x 104	36 x 75	66 x 90
9 x 76 (twin)	72 x 104	39 x 76	66 x 90
9 x 80 (twin long)	72 x 115	39 x 80	66 x 90
8 x x76 (¾ bed)	72 x 104	48 x 76	72 x 90
4 x 76 (double)	81 x 104	54 x 76	80 x 90
4 x 80 (double long)	81 x 115	54 x 80	80 x 90
0 x 80 (queen)	90 x 115	60 x 80	90 x 90
2 x 84 (king)	100 x 115	72 x 84	108 x 90
5 x 80 (king)	108 x 115	76 x 80	108 x 90
8 x 76 (dual twin)	108 x 115	76 x 80	108 x 90
8 x 80 (long dual twin)	108 x 115	78 x 80	108 x 90
8 x 84 (extra long dual twin)	108 x 115	78 x 84	108 x 90

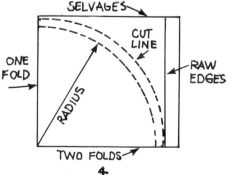

4

mail order sources

FOR SHOPPING BY CATALOGUE AND DECORATING INFORMATION

(Please write directly to the sources, not to the publisher or authors. Where no charge is listed, catalogue is free.)

For further information about any Sears, Roebuck merchandise seen in the pages of this book write to:

Sears, Roebuck and Company
P.O. Box 11787
Chicago, Illinois 60611

From page 70
Easy Edges
501 Madison Avenue
New York, New York 10022

At: Bloomingdale's
May Company—all stores
Petersen's, Arlington Heights, Illinois

From page 71
Environmental Concepts
9100 Wilshire Boulevard
Beverly Hills, California 90212

At: Bloomingdale's
May Company—all stores
Filene's, Boston
Joseph Magnin

REPRODUCTIONS OF PERIOD FURNITURE

American, English and French:

Hunt Galleries
2920 N. Center Street
Hickory, North Carolina 28601
Catalogue $1.00

Ephraim Marsh
Box 266
Concord, ·North Carolina 28025
Catalogue 25¢

Bryan Robeson
Box 757
Hickory, North Carolina 28601
Catalogue 25¢

English and French:

Allen Upholstery
515 New Street
Allentown, Pennsylvania 18102

French and Mediterranean:

White of Mebane
Mebane, North Carolina 27302
Catalogue 50¢

Victorian:

Martha M. House
1022 S. Decatur Street
Montgomery, Alabama 36104
Catalogue $1.00

Magnolia House
726 Andover
Atlanta, Georgia 30327
Catalogue $1.00

Early American:

Yield House
North Conway, New Hampshire 03860

Americana:

Heritage House
Chadds Ford, Pennsylvania 19317

BUTCHER BLOCK FURNITURE

J. & D. Brauner, Inc.
298 Bowery
New York, New York 10012
Catalogue 50¢

The Butcher Block People
The Schoenheit Company
1660 S. Clinton
Chicago, Illinois 60616
Catalogue 50¢

The Woodshed
315 Sunrise Highway
Lynbrook, New York 11563
Catalogue 50¢

MODERN FURNITURE

J. Carlton's, Inc.
176 Madison Avenue
New York, New York 10016

Design Fair
287 Bloomfield
Verona, New Jersey 07044

Geneda Imports (Danish modern)
P.O. Box 204
Teaneck, New Jersey 07666
Catalogue 25¢

Leathercrafter
303 East 51st Street
New York, New York 10022
Catalogue 50¢

UNFINISHED, READY-TO-FINISH, KITS AND KNOCKED-DOWN FURNITURE

Artistic Frame International Ltd. (chair frames)
407–13 East 91st Street
New York, New York 10028
Catalogue $1.50

Cohasset Colonials (ready-to-finish kits of
    Early American pieces)
472 Ship Street
Cohasset, Massachusetts 02025
Catalogue 50¢

DCA Home Furnishings (Fastcube assemblies)
4865 Stenton Avenue
Philadelphia, Pennsylvania 19144

Door Store (unfinished and finished furniture)
3140 M Street NW
Washington, D.C. 20007
Catalogue $1.00

Furn-a-Kit (knocked-down furniture)
140 East Union Avenue
East Rutherford, New Jersey 07073
Catalogue $1.00

Furniture-in-the-Raw
1015 Second Avenue
New York, New York 10022

Marion Travis (ready-to-finish or prefinished
    Americana)
P.O. Box 292
Statesville, North Carolina 28677
Catalogue 25¢

The Workbench
470 Park Avenue South
New York, New York 10016
Catalogue $1.00

WICKER AND ALUMINUM FURNITURE

Basket House (wicker furniture)
89 W. Main Street
Rockaway, New Jersey 07866
Catalogue 25¢

J. F. Day & Co. (cast aluminum)
2820 6th Avenue South
Birmingham, Alabama 35233
Catalogue 25¢

The Patio (tubular aluminum)
P.O. Box 2843
San Francisco, California 94126

Wicker Garden
400 Jacksonville Road
Hatboro, Pennsylvania 19040
Catalogue 25¢

FABRICS, READY-MADES, WINDOW TREATMENTS

Country Curtains (unbleached muslin curtains)
Stockbridge, Massachusetts 01262

Grillion Corp. (precut plywood grille panels)
189 First Street
Brooklyn, New York 11215
Catalogue $1.00

Gurian's (Indian crewel fabrics and ready-mades)
11 East 33rd Street
New York, New York 10016
Catalogue $1.00

Homespun House (made-to-measure curtains
    and do-it-yourself seamless draperies)
9038 Lindblade
Culver City, California 90230
Catalogue 25¢

Old Colony Curtains (ready-mades, canopies,
    swage, tiers)
Box 787
Westfield, New Jersey 07090

Ronnie Drapery Corp. (made-to-measure
    curtains, bedspreads)
145 Broad Avenue
Fairview, New Jersey 07022

J. Schachter Corp. (ready-made spreads, quilts,
    pillows, blankets)
115 Allen Street
New York, New York 10002
Catalogue 50¢

Town & Country Workshop (fabric frames for
    windows)
219 N. Carpenter
Chicago, Illinois 60607

RUGS

Chas. W. Jacobsen, Inc. (oriental rugs)
401 S. Salina Street
Syracuse, New York 13201

Safari Skins, Ltd. (fake fur rugs)
Box 4156
San Rafael, California 94903

Skon(rya rug kits)
53 Lambert Lane
New Rochelle, New York 10804
Catalogue $1.00

Evelyn Ulrich's Rug Hanging Kit
Rochman Imports, Inc.
102 West 75th Street, Room 70
New York, New York 10026

DECORATING INFORMATION AND IDEAS FOR WINDOWS

The Decorative Window Shade
Window Shade Manufacturers Association
230 Park Avenue
New York, New York 10017
Booklet 25¢

Do-It-Yourself Ideas for Window Shades
Window Shade Manufacturers Association
230 Park Avenue
New York, New York 10017
Booklet 25¢

How to Create Your Own Beautiful Window Fashions
Graber Company
Graber Plaza
Middleton, Wisconsin 53562
Booklet $1.00

How to Make Your Windows Beautiful
Kirsch Company
Sturgis, Michigan 40991
Catalogue $1.00

Window Magic with Levolor Blinds and Shades
Levolor Lorentzen, Inc.
720 Monroe Street
Hoboken, New Jersey 07030

Window Shade Parade
Breneman, Inc.
1133 Sycamore
Cincinnati, Ohio 45210
Booklet 75¢

WALLS

Fingertip Decorating (with spray paint, tape and press-on vinyl)
Borden Chemical, Division of Borden, Inc.
50 West Broad Street
Columbus, Ohio 43215
Send stamped, self-addressed business envelope (#10)

Instant Decorating Ideas
Bassett Mirror Company, Department 72-A
Bassett, Virginia 24055
Booklet 50¢

Living Walls by Claire M. Barrows
The Wallcoverings Council
969 Third Avenue
New York, New York 10021
Paperback book 95¢

Supergraphics
Environmental Graphics
c/o Pandora Productions, Inc.
1117 Vicksburg Lane North
Wayzata, Minnesota 55391

Syroco (wall accessories)
Syracuse, New York 13201
Catalogue $1.00

25 Quick Ways to Beautify Your Rooms with Con-Tact
Comark Plastics
1407 Broadway
New York, New York 10018

U.S. Plywood: 6 idea booklets for den-library, family room, kitchen, bedroom, dining room, living room
Box 61
New York, New York 10046

Wallcoverings and You
United-DeSoto
3101 South Kedzie Avenue
Chicago, Illinois 60623
Booklet 25¢

Wall Story (vinyl wallcoverings)
General Tire & Rubber Co.
P.O. Box 951
Akron, Ohio 44329
Booklet 50¢

LIGHTING

A Lamp Is to Light
Robert Sonneman Associates, Inc.
37–50 57th Street
Woodside, New York 11377
Booklet 25¢

The Light Book: How To Be at Home with Lighting
General Electric Enquiry Bureau Department 482
Nela Park
Cleveland, Ohio 44118

656 Ideas for Decorating with Lighting
Progress Lighting
Box 12701
Philadelphia, Pennsylvania 19134
Booklet 50¢

FLOORS

Ceramic Tile Makes a Lot of Sense
Tile Council of America, Inc.
P.O. Box 2222, Room 206
Princeton, New Jersey 08540
Booklet 50¢

Great Beginnings (color schemes with carpets)
Bigelow
Box 161
Whitestone, New York 11357
Booklet 25¢

How to Buy a Floor, A Complete Guide to the Selection of Resilient Flooring for the Home
Armstrong Cork Company
7204 Maple Avenue
Lancaster, Pennsylvania 17604

Peel & Stick Tiles
Flintkote
East Rutherford, New Jersey 07073

BATHROOMS

Bathroom Ideas
Kohler Company
Department B
Kohler, Wisconsin 53044
Booklet 50¢

Splash of Summer Sunshine
Eljer Plumbingware
3 Gateway Center
Pittsburgh, Pennsylvania 15222

FURNITURE

Album of Furniture Classics
Johnson Wax Consumer Education
1525 Howe Street
Racine, Wisconsin 53403

Ethan Allen Treasury of American Traditional
Interiors
Baumritter Corporation
Attention: S. Pearl
205 Lexington Avenue
New York, New York 10016
358 page book $5.00

Discover the Wonderful World of You
Bassett Furniture
Bassett, Virginia 24055
Booklet 50¢

Hide-A-Bed Sofas
Simmons Company
2 Park Avenue
New York, New York 10016
Booklet 25¢

Know How to Buy Home Furnishings
Consumer Information Department
The Brand Names Foundation, Inc.
477 Madison Avenue
New York, New York 10022
Booklet 50¢

Tender, Loving Care
Drexel Furniture
Drexel, North Carolina 28619
Booklet $1.00

REMODELING

Decorating Ideas
PPG Industries, Inc.
1 Gateway Center
Pittsburgh, Pennsylvania 15222
Booklet 25¢

How to Install Factory-Finished Paneling
Georgia-Pacific Corp.
Attention: R. E. Perdue
900 S.W. Fifth Avenue
Portland, Oregon 97204
Booklet 25¢

Ideas Galore
U. S. Plywood
Department IDEA, Attention: N. Stuart
777 Third Avenue
New York, New York 10017
Booklet 25¢

Ideas for Remodeling
American Plywood Association
(Form 70-635)
1119 A Street
Tacoma, Washington 98401
Booklet 50¢

DECORATING WITH SHEETS, TRIMS AND FABRICS

Buying and Care of Towels and Sheets
Cannon Homemaking Service
P.O. Box 107
Kannapolis, North Carolina 20801
Booklet 25¢

Primer for Tie-Dying Fabrics
Rit Dye
P.O. Box 307
Coventry, Connecticut 06238

Start with a Sheet
Burlington Industries
P.O. Box 262
Brooklyn, New York 11223

Tricks with Trim
Conso Products
P.O. Box 325
New York, New York 10010
Booklet 10¢

FURNITURE REFINISHING

Antiquing Made Easy
Martin-Senour
2500 S. Senour Avenue
Chicago, Illinois 60608
Booklet 25¢

Tips on Wood Finishing
Minwax Company
72 Oak Street
Clifton, New Jersey 07014

further readings

DECORATING AND REMODELING IDEAS

Decorating Room by Room, Ellen J. Levine, Pyramid, 1970.
Decorating Small Apartments, Olga Steir and J. E. Schuler, William Morrow, 1969.
Easy Steps to Successful Decorating, Barbara Taylor Bradford, Simon and Schuster, 1971.
Elegant Decorating on a Limited Budget, Janet A. Reis, Macmillan, 1965.
Groovy Guide to Decorating Your Room (paperback), A. and Luciana Parks, New American Library, 1971.
House & Garden's Complete Guide to Decoration, Simon and Schuster, 1970.
Kitchens and Dining Rooms, Mary Gilliat, Viking Press, 1970.
Remodeling Your Home (paperback), Sunset Magazine Editors, Lane, 1969.
Starting from Scratch (paperback), Joanna Barnes, Tower, 1970.
You and Your Apartment, Carlton Varney, Bobbs-Merrill, 1967.
Young Designs in Living, Barbara Plumb, Viking Press, 1969.

HELP IN BUYING

How to Buy at Auction, Michael De Forrest, Simon and Schuster, 1972.
How to Buy Furniture, Donna Difloe, Macmillan, 1972.

HOW TO MAKE, RESTORE, REFINISH OR PAINT FURNITURE

All About Antiquing and Restoring Furniture, Robert Berger, Hawthorne, 1972.
The Art of the Painted Finish for Furniture and Decoration, Isabel O'Neil, William Morrow, 1971.
Cabinet Making for Beginners, Charles H. Hayward, Drake Publishers, 1971.
Designer Furniture Anyone Can Make, William E. Schremp, Simon and Schuster, 1972.
How to Paint Anything, The Complete Guide to Painting and Refinishing, Hubbard H. Cobb, Macmillan, 1972.
Practical Upholstery, C. Howes, Drake Publishers, 1971.
Reproducing Antique Furniture: Construction, Hardware, Finishing, Franklin H. Gottshall, Crown, 1971.

CRAFTS TO DO AT HOME

Art and Craft of Hand Weaving: Including Fabric Design, Lili Blumenau, Crown, 1955.
Art of Weaving, Elsa Regensteiner, Van Nostrand Reinhold, 1970.
The Complete Book of Sewing, Constance Talbot and Isabelle Stevenson, Crown, 1972.
Fun with Crewel Embroidery, Erica Wilson, Charles Scribner's Sons, 1965.
Macramé: Creative Design in Knotting, Donna Z. Meilach, Crown, 1971.
Manning on Decoupage, Hiram Manning, Hearthside Press, 1971.
Needlepoint, Hope Hanley, Charles Scribner's Sons, 1964.
Needlepoint Designs, Louis J. Gartner, Jr., William Morrow, 1971.
A New Look at Needlepoint, Carol Cheney Rome and Georgia French Devlin, Crown, 1972.
Patchwork Crochet, Jackie Shapiro and Her Mother, Workman, 1972.
Plastics for the Craftsman: Basic Techniques for Working with Plastics, Jay Hartley Newman and Lee Scott Newman, Crown, 1972.
Gloria Vanderbilt's Book of Collage, Van Nostrand Reinhold, 1970.

HOW TO KNOW ANTIQUES, PERIODS AND STYLES IN FURNISHINGS

Antiques Past and Present, Katharine Morrison McClinton, Crown, 1971.
Decorating Defined, José Wilson and Arthur Leaman, Simon and Schuster, 1970.
The Dictionary of Antiques and the Decorative Arts, Louise and H. B. Boger, Charles Scribner's Sons, 1957.
How to Know American Antiques (paperback), Alice Winchester, New American Library, 1951.
How to Know French Antiques, Ruth Costantino, Signet Books, New American Library, 1961.
New Encyclopedia of Furniture, Joseph Aronson, Crown, 1967.
The New York Times Book of Antiques, Marvin Schwartz and Betsy Wade, Quadrangle Books, 1972.
An Outline of Period Furniture, Katharine Morrison McClinton, Clarkson N. Potter, Inc., 1972.

index